At-Tawhid

Monotheism

Ayatullah Muhammad-Taqi
Misbah Yazdi

Copyright

Copyright © 2022 al-Burāq Publications.

All rights reserved. No part of this publication may be reproduced, distributed, or transmitted in any form or by any means, including photocopying, recording, or other electronic or mechanical methods, without the prior written permission of the publisher, except in the case of brief quotations embodied in critical reviews and certain other noncommercial uses permitted by copyright law. For permission requests, write to the publisher, addressed "Attention: Permissions [At-Tawhid: Monotheism]," at the email address below.

ISBN: 978-1-956276-03-9

Printed and published by al-Burāq Publications.

Ordering Information
We offer discounts and promotions for wholesale purchases and for non-profit organizations, libraries, and other educational institutions. Contact us at the email below for further information.

www.al-Buraq.org
publications@al-Buraq.org

This printed edition | January 2022

Dedication

The publication of this book was made possible through the generous support of our donors.

Please recite *Sūrah al-Fātiha* and ask Allāh for the Divine reward (*thawāb*) to be conferred upon the donors and also the souls of all the deceased in whose memory their loved ones have contributed graciously towards the publication of *At-Tawhid: Monotheism.*

Duaa al-Hujja

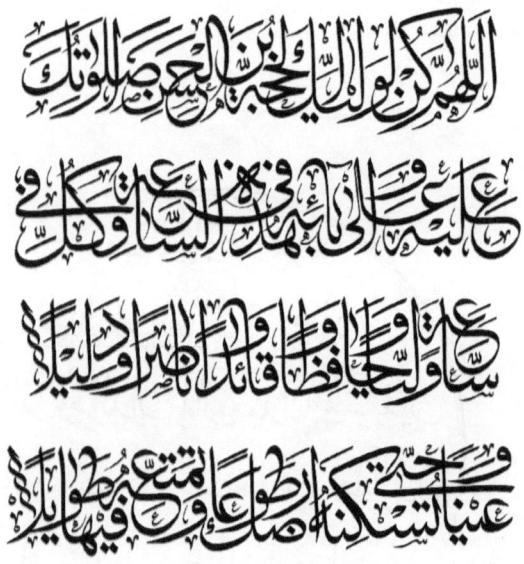

O Allah, be, for Your representative, the Hujjat (proof), son of al-Hasan, Your blessings be upon him and his forefathers, in this hour and in every hour: a guardian, a protector, a leader, a helper, a proof, and an eye - until You make him live on the Earth, in obedience (to You), and cause him to live in it for a long time.

Table of Contents

Preface...9

Part 1: At-Tawhid in the Value System of Islam 13

    At-Tawhid (Monotheism) - The Base of Divine Religions 13

    The Necessity & Significance of At-Tawhid to Al-A'immatul
        Ma'sumuun (The Twelve Infallible Imams)......................14

    The Hadith Bearing Silsilatu-dhab..15

    The Statement Made by Amirul-Mu'mineen al-Imam 'Ali (A.S.) on
        the Battle of al-Jamal...17

    At-Tawhid - The Root of All Beliefs..19

    Description of the Relationship Between At-Tawhid and the Other
        Beliefs...21

    The Two Ideological and Value Systems of Islam and Their
        Relationship..22

    The Relationship of At-Tawhid With Other Principles of the
        Religion...25

    The Relationship of Tawhid with Adl..27

    The Relationship of at-Tawhid with Nubuwwah 29

    The Relationship of at-Tawhid with Ma'ad 30

    At-Tawhid - The Pivot of the Value System (of Islam).............32

    Can at-Tawhid be Found by Education?...................................35

    At-Tawhid in Creation 36

    At-Tawhid in Rububiyyah (Lordship).......................................38

    Rububiyyah Pertaining to Divine Laws....................................40

Quranic Ayah in Regard to Rububiyyah Pertaining to Creation .43

The Position of Lordship in Divine Legislation and the Required Level of at-Tawhid..44

At-Tawhid in Ubudiyyah (Servitude) to Allah 49

Manifestations in At-Tawhid in Ubudiyyah to Allah.................52

The Reality of At-Tawhid 58

Expression of At-Tawhid With the Tongue and Not Out of Conviction 60

Obligation to at-Tawhid...63

The Meaning of the Term At-Tawhid and the Initiation of Distortion in It...64

Wrong Imaginations Concerning the Meaning of At-Tawhid..68

The Subject of Bada' 73

Clarification of Mechanical and Dynamic Movements..............74

Divine Management..84

Divine Wilayah 88

At-Tawhid in Guidance...96

The Guidance Particular to Man..103

Providing Sustenance..110

Allah's Predestination in Men's Sustenance 115

Reasons For and Causes of Change of Subsistence 118

Providing Sustenance Through Uncommon Ways..................125

Divine Wisdom..127

The Wisdom Behind Bearing Difficulties by Man 129

Divine Qada' (Destiny) and Qadr (Decree) 143

    Correct Clarification of the Meaning of Divine Qada' and Qadr 145

Part 2: At-Tawhid in the Ideological System of Islam. 159

The Concept of Value 159

Man's Honor 160

    Moral Value 163

The Criterion for Moral Value 166

The Value of Freedom 169

Commitment and Sense of Duty 171

Taqwa 173

    Stages of Taqwa 183

    The Relationship of Taqwa with At-Tawhid 187

Ibadah (Worship to Allah) 193

    The Basis of Responsibility 195

    Creational and Divine Legislative 'Ibadah 197

    Criticism on A Theory 203

    Clarification of the Ethical Theory of Islam 206

    The First Principle 208

    Clarification of the Criterion for the Good and the Bad 215

    The Second Principle 217

    Various Meanings and Cases of the Application of Qurb 218

    The First Matter 224

    The Second Matter 224

    The Third Principle 227

Quranic Expressions About the Philosophy of Morality 229

Preface

بِسْمِ اللهِ الرَّحْمٰنِ الرَّحِيْمِ

In the Name of Allāh, the Most Gracious, the Most Merciful

The Establishment and Stability of the Islamic system requires, more than anything else, the firmness of the beliefs and values of Islam in the hearts of the people. The realization of this very significant matter, in its own turn, depends upon the universality of Islamic education at different levels, by using multifarious means and opportunities. One of the best of such occasions and opportunities is the weekly congregations of Salatul-Jumu'ah (Friday Prayer), particularly in cities where the proceedings of the Salatul-Jumu'ah are directly broadcast by the radio and television.

Hence, in response to the request of the management committee, in charge of the affairs of the Salatul-Jumu'ah in the city of Tehran, I delivered a series of lectures on "The status of At-Tawhid in the ideological system and value system of Islam". The texts of these lectures were regularly published in the Persian language daily, viz: "Jamhuriyyi-Islami (The Islamic Republic)."

Now, responding to the requests made by a large number of the listeners and also by some friends, an abridged version of these lectures is being published for the interested readers. It is hoped that this humble service will please Al-Imam Muhammad Al-Mahdi (AS)-may Allah the Almighty hasten his auspicious reappearance.

Muhammad-Taqi Misbah Yazdi

Part 1: At-Tawhid in the Value System of Islam

In the Name of Allāh, the Most Gracious, the Most Merciful

At-Tawhid (Monotheism) - The Base of Divine Religions

The matter to be discussed here is the system of At-Tawhid in the ideological system and value system of Islam which constitutes the main base of divine religions, in particular, the sacred religion of Islam.

The Holy Qur'an says:

> "And certainly We raised in every people a Messenger saying: 'Serve Allah and shun the shaytan'... (16:36)."

Another ayah (verse of the Holy Qur'an) says:

> "And We did not send before you any Messenger but We revealed to him that there is no god but Me, therefore, serve Me (21:25)"

Also, each and every one of Allah's Prophets (AS), as mentioned in the Holy Qur'an, from the very outset of their being appointed as a Prophet by Allah, said to their people:

"... 'O my people! Serve Allah, you have no god other than Him'... (7:59)."

Also, the Holy Prophet (SA) of Islam, at the time of his Al-Bi'thatun-Nabawiyyah (the appointment by Allah as His Prophet) said:

"Say there is no god but Allah so that you will find salvation."

Prosperity, salvation and felicity both in this world and in the Hereafter depend upon and are to be sought in At-Tawhid. So, believe in Allah- the One and bear witness to His Oneness so that you will achieve salvation.

The Necessity & Significance of At-Tawhid to Al-A'immatul Ma'sumuun (The Twelve Infallible Imams)

Besides, it has been narrated from the Infallible Imams (AS), in various forms that the felicity both in this world and the Hereafter are to be found in At-Tawhid. One of such ahadith (traditions) is the following:

"The formula: *'La ilaha illallah'* (meaning there is no god but Allah) is the price of paradise."[1]

---

[1] Ash-Shaykh As-Saduq, "At-Tawhid", p. 21, Riwayah No 13.

Also, there are many other ahadith in our books on ahadith indicating that if a person is a muwahhid (monotheist, believer in One God) and preserves the belief in At-Tawhid till the end of his life, he will be protected against and immune from Allah's torment.

The Hadith Bearing Silsilatu-dhab

Hadrat Ali ibn Musa ar-Rida (AS) - The Eighth Infallible Imam- in the hadith bearing silsilatu-dhab (golden chain of Infallible narrators), which he narrated among a gathering of twelve thousand men of learning and 'Ulama' (Islamic scholars) of the city of Nayshapur and in the social and political conditions prevailing at that time, when he said: "I heard from my father. Musa ibn Ja'far (AS) who narrated from his father and forefathers (AS) reaching to 'Amirul-Mu'mineen (The Commander of the Faithful), Al-Imam 'Ali (AS) who narrated from the Holy Prophet (SA) of Islam, who narrated the same from Jibra'il (the archangel Gabriel) saying that Allah says,"

"The words *'La ilaha illallah'* (there is no god but Allah) is My Fortress, so anybody who entered my fortress became immune from my torment."[2]

---

[2] "Uyun Akhbarir-Rida", vol.1, p. 135; Ash-Shaykh As-Saduq, "At-Tawhid", p. 24, Riwayah No. 21.

At-Tawhid: Monotheism

So, the words *'La ilaha illallah'* and bearing witness to At-Tawhid (to the Oneness of Allah) and belief in Allah The Almighty is the firm Fortress of the Almighty Allah and the one who believes in At-Tawhid and hears witness to the Oneness of Allah has entered this firm Fortress and will be immune from Allah's torment.

In a number of riwayat, it has been said that anybody who utters these words of At-Tawhid sincerely, will enter the Paradise, According to the Imam (AS), the sincere believing in At-Tawhid is to avoid disobedience to Allah- The One. Anyhow, the riwayat it concerning At-Tawhid are many and the 'ulama' and great men of religious learning's have written special books in this connection based on the sayings of the Holy Prophet (SA) of Islam and the Infallible Imams (AS) which form an invaluable treasure.

Here, a question arises and that is what role does belief in At-Tawhid and in the Oneness of Allah play in man's individual and social life and that why this subject has so much been emphasized by Allah's Prophets (AS), so much so that they have unanimously put it at the head of their call (to Allah) and that the Holy Prophet (SA) of Islam and the Infallible Imams (AS) have made utmost efforts and borne many sufferings to clarify it and clarify the dimensions it has.

The Statement Made by Amirul-Mu'mineen al-Imam 'Ali (A.S.) on the Battle of al-Jamal

During the Battle of Al-Jamal, a Bedouin Arab said: "I want to talk to Amirul-Mu'mineen (AS)". He was taken to Amirul-Mu'mineen (AS). Those who were around Al-Imam, 'Ali (AS), his Companions and the army commanders, were looking forward to see what matters that Bedouin Arab had to discuss with Imam (AS) in that critical situation? Had he got some information about the war? Had he got any secret news? What kind of matter it is? While they were all waiting, that Bedouin Arab suddenly raised the subject of Al-Tawhid, saying:

"Do you say that indeed Allah is One?"

Imam (AS)'s companions objected to him, saying: "Is it the proper time for such talks? Don't you see that Amirul-Mu'mineen (AS) is busy in handling the affairs of the war?" Thus they attempted to take him away from Imam (AS) and hinder him from continuing his talk. However, the Imam said:

At-Tawhid: Monotheism

"Let him speak, what this Bedouin is seeking is the very thing we demand from these people whom we are fighting with."[3]

Imam Ali (AS) meant that the war was for At-Tawhid. Then, in that very battlefield and in those very conditions and circumstances, Al- Imam 'Ali (AS) made certain remarks about At-Tawhid which have been recorded in the books on riwayat, and which arc difficult to be understood even by us- the educated ones.

By citing the above example, we mean to point out that the matter of At-Tawhid has been of such a great significance to the Leaders of the religion of Islam and all the great Prophets (A.S.) that they did not want to miss any opportunity for paying attention to it, even in the Battle of Al-Jamal which was being fought against a number of so-called Muslims and muwahiddin.

Hence, this fundamental principle should be imprinted on the minds of the people more and more and in a better way and the Muslims should acquire acquaintance with all its dimensions so that it affects the felicity of people in both this world and the Hereafter. If At-Tawhid is known, as it should be, and penetrates into hearts, men's life will become

---

[3] Ash-Shaykh As-Saduq, "At-Tawhid", p. 83.

totally divine and will be placed in the right direction, on the straight path and towards the Almighty Allah and will remain immune from deviational trends, errors and blunders which are all rooted in deviation from At-Tawhid.

The introduction will hopefully serve to clarify the significance of this matter from the view point of Islam and all other divine religions; and, no doubt, this belief can guarantee man's attitude towards the world of creation and also man's conduct towards his perfection. But how?

At-Tawhid - The Root of All Beliefs

In short, we believe that At-Tawhid is the root of all Haqq (true) beliefs and the root of all values and we have no doubt in this regard. However, the question may arise as to how this matter should be expressed so that it may be proved that At-Tawhid is the basis of all the true beliefs and the basis of all the right values and how anybody who becomes a believer in At-Tawhid will become an inmate of Paradise and will he blessed with felicity both in this world and in the Hereafter?

In the Holy Qur'an, there is a very interesting and valuable parable which we would quote here to clarify the relationship of At-Tawhid with the ideological system and the value system of Islam. The Holy Qur'an says:

"Have you not considered how Allah has set a parable of a good word (being) like a good tree, whose root is firm and whose branches are in heaven (14:24)."

Such a tree will invariably bear sweet and delicious fruits of its own. However, the word which has no stable root and which is not based on the firm and solid pillars of the truth and (he reality is the parable of a tree whose root has been pulled out of the ground. Such a tree will obviously not only bear no fruit, but will before long decay and be destroyed too, as says the Holy Qur'an:

"And the parable of an evil word is as an evil tree pulled up from the earth's surface; it has no stability (14:26)."

In this Quranic parable, the Islamic system has been regarded as a tree whose root is "Al-Kalimatu tayyibah" (The Holy Kalimah) word, i.e., "La ilaha illallah" (meaning there is no god but Allah). This word and this belief is a firm root which becomes established in the hearts of the talented men and which generates other roots as well.

With the growth of this root and tree, many branches leaves grow and these will eventually bear blossoms, flowers and delicious and valuable fruits. And the difference between this tree and the other trees is that the other trees bear fruit only in particular seasons of the year, but this tree never ceases to bear fruit and invariably puts its fruit at the disposal of men, which fruit is nothing other than felicity both in this world and in the Hereafter.

"Yielding its fruit in every season by the permission of its Lord... (14:25)."

Description of the Relationship Between At-Tawhid and the Other Beliefs

By deriving inspiration from this Holy ayah of the Holy Qur'an, we can attempt to clarify the matter as to what relation exists between Al-Tawhid and the other beliefs and also between At-Tawhid and the value system of Islam.

Fortunately, unlike many of the schools of thought which on the basis of detective thoughts, put together some elements and without having considered any relationship between those principles and elements, say: "This ideology as a whole is comprised by a number of principles", the whole system of the religion of Islam is a coherent, well-knitted and harmonious system of which all the elements are related to each other and among which there is no disharmony.

The Two Ideological and Value Systems of Islam and Their Relationship

As a whole, the content of the religion of Islam can be regarded as a two-part system and two secondary systems which are interrelated and united together, and which constitute the whole Islamic system. One is the system of the beliefs and the other is the system of the values, In Islam, there are a series of beliefs in which the people should believe, accept and have faith in and there are a series of values which they should observe in their actions and behavior.

We call the former part 'the ideological system' and the latter 'the value system' of Islam, and by deriving inspiration from the holy verse regarding ash- shujarutul-tayyibah (the good tree, The Holy Qur'an, Surah 14, Ayah 24), we can interpret the former part as usul'ud-Din (The fundamental principles of Islam) and the latter part as furu'ud-Din (the duties to be performed according to Islamic Shari'ath).

For men's lives, the beliefs arc like the root of a tree which, if arc firm in people's hearts, will also affect their actions, provided that they have adequate awareness and insight about those and properly know all the dimensions of beliefs.

So, in the first place, the beliefs should be strengthened and made firm; and in the second place, attention should be paid to their practical effects; because though the system of Islam is comprised by two systems, yet between them there exists a relationship to the similar relationship between asl (root or principle) and far' (the branch), the relationship between the root and the branches and leaves. Hence the Islamic scholars have called the true beliefs as usul'ud- Din and the value system (as the furu'ud- Din). The former (the principles) are the roots of the tree of Islam and the latter (the values) are the branches of the tree of Islam.

On the other hand, there is mutual (relation of) affecting and being affected between the root (on one hand) and the branches and the leaves (on the other). Both the 'root' has a vital role in a tree's growth and in its development of branches and leaves and also the 'branches and the leaves' have a considerable effect on the strength of the root. So, just as in the beginning the roots cause the emergence of the branches and the leaves, the latter, too, in their turn help the root to gain strength.

In other words: the curve of the relation between the root and the branch and their changes is the form of zigzag, in the way that from the root it goes towards the branch and again from the branch it returns to the root and in this way this current between the 'root', namely, the faith or belief and the 'branch', namely, the action will continue, the stronger the faith, the stronger and more effects it will have in action; and in the same way, the more a man observes the laws (the branches) of the religion and acts in accordance with his root belief, the more will the root of his belief be strengthened. This is a mutual affecting and being affected (relation) between the root on one hand and the branches and the leaves on the other, between faith and action, between worldview and ideology. However, it is basically the worldview which evolves the ideology.

If we ponder carefully about the above-mentioned ayat of the Holy Quran' an, once again this relation will be clear to us. In the Holy Qur'an, Allah (SWT) says:

"And we did not send before you any Messenger but We revealed to him that there is no god but Me... (21:25)."

And then Allah expresses the branch attached to the above principle: " ... therefore serve Me.", That is now that you know that Allah is the One and none other than Him in the world has this position, so you should serve Me (Allah-The One). Serving (or worshiping) concerns the action and knowing that Allah is one, causes man to attempt to serve (worship) Him in action. If that base does not exist, there will not be any room for this branch and if that root is not firm, this branch will not bear fruit.

To avoid getting away from the subject, we should mention that the theme of our discussion is the expression of the status of At-Tawhid in the ideological system and value system of Islam, that is, in that collection of beliefs and values in which a Muslim should believe and which he should observe in action, what position does At-Tawhid have and what role does it play?

The Relationship of At-Tawhid With Other Principles of the Religion

If we regard At-Tawhid just as this very simple and common concept which we have learned in religious schools, though it is true, yet it does not suffice to clarify this relation. We have learned that the first Asl (principle) of the principles of the religion of Islam is that Allah (SWT) is one and not two; that the second principle is that the Prophets (AS) have been truthfully appointed by Allah (SWT) to guide the people; that the third principle is belief in Ma'ad (the resurrection): that the fourth principle is that Allah (SWT) is just and that the fifth principle is that the successor of the Holy Prophet (SA) of Islam is the Ma'sum (Infallible) Imam who has been appointed by Allah (SWT).

If we measure these concepts as described, we will see no relation among them, for example, between the belief that Allah is One and the belief that men will he revived on the Resurrection Day. This thought of lack of relation which at first occurs to the simple-minded persons, is because At- Tawhid has not been properly understood (by them). To clarify the relation of these principles with At-Tawhid, we need to expand these relations to some extent, so that it will become clearly known that how by uttering *"La ilaha illallah"* (there is no god but Allah), man's felicity both in this world and the hereafter will be secured.

The great Islamic scholar and commentator of the Holy Qur'an -the late Allah Tabataba'i (may Allah bless his soul) says: At-Tawhid, when expanded, becomes the whole of Islam, and Islam, when condensed, At-Tawhid is acquired."

At-Tawhid is like a compressed treasure which on the surface appears like a simple ideological principle, but which however, when, expanded and spread, embraces the whole of Islam. In other words, the whole of Islam is as a body which is formed by various limbs and parts and of which the soul is At-Tawhid. If At-Tawhid, namely, the soul is breathed into this body, it will be a body which is alive, otherwise it will turn into a lifeless and dead system. The Holy Qur'an has also a comparison in this connection, it says:

"... a good word (being) like a good tree, whose root is firm and whose branches are in heaven (14:24)."

At-Tawhid is as the root and base of the religion.

The Relationship of Tawhid with Adl

With the above introduction, we compare the relationship of each of the beliefs (the principles of religion) with At-Tawhid: We know that the Almighty Allah is unique in all perfections; but the uniqueness (oneness) does not mean the uniqueness (or oneness) which may be attributed to His creatures, i.e., every being in this world is one, or as the philosophers say: unity is integrated with the being (wherever there is a true unity, there is a true being, and wherever there is a true being, there is unity).

This is the same misconception about the wrongness of which Amirul-Mu'mineen Al-Imam Ali (AS) expressed to that Bedouin Arab in the Battle of Al-Jamal. By saying that man or any other being is one, it is meant that for him (or for the existence of it) two, three or thousands of other beings can also he imagined. But Allah (SWT) has such Oneness (or uniqueness) that it is impossible to imagine a second or a number two for Him and in this same concept His uniqueness or oneness in all His perfections is conceived.

That is, no one's power is like Allah's, wherever there is a power, it is from Him. That is to say, other than Allah (SWT), no one has any power or any knowledge of his own, wherever there is knowledge, it is from Allah (SWT); wherever there is life, it is from Allah (SWT); wherever there is perfection and beauty, it is from Allah (SWT).

If we understand the fact that the Almighty Allah possesses each and every perfection of being infinite, we will know that no imperfection can be imagined for Him. And naturally such a One, Who is the very perfection and from whom every perfection emanates and stems, does not perform any action which does not cause any perfection and which does not lead to the emergence of perfection and also His aim of the creation of His creatures is nothing other than their perfection and eternal salvation.

And, He is also devoid of oppression which is a behavior away from perfection and will treat each and every individual on the basis of 'adl (Justice) and fairness. So we see that the second principle of the principles of the religion, namely, 'adl has direct relation with At-Tawhid and knowing the Oneness of Allah (SWT).

The Relationship of at-Tawhid with Nubuwwah

Nubuwwah (Prophethood), too, has such a relationship. If you invite a guest to your house and insistently ask him to be your guest today, but do not give him the address of your house, you have quite obviously not done a wise act. Can it really be said that you desire to have the person as your guest while you have not shown him the way.

If a person seriously means to be a host, he will certainly give the would-be-guest the address of his house and will even warn the guest of the mistakes which may possibly occur due to the resemblance of the alleys and this is a wise act. Allah (SWT), too, has created men so that they will attain eternal felicity.

Therefore, as His wisdom demands, Allah (SWT) should appoint Prophets (AS) to guide His creatures, show them the way, keep them away from mistakes and errors and hence it is again knowing Allah which leads us to (the knowledge of) Nubuwwah (Prophethood).

In the wake of the proof of sending the Prophets (AS), Divine Wisdom demands that after the demise of Allah's (Last) prophet (SA), Prophet Muhammad (SA) - The Holy Prophet (SA) of Islam, people will not be left without a leader and guide and will know whom to refer to when encountering with problems.

Thus the matter of Imamah (succession of Prophet Muhammad (SA) by the Twelve Infallible Imams (AS)) is realized.

The Relationship of at-Tawhid with Ma'ad

After the way (to Allah) has been clarified, the people either traverse the way exactly as the prophets (AS) and their successors (AS) have illustrated and follow the same path which they have directed, or they deviate from that way. It will be away from Justice and wise conduct if these two groups, (namely, those who have traversed that straight way, have overlooked their desires and lusts and have sacrificed their lives in the way of the exaltation of the words of At-Tawhid on one hand, and those who have fought against them (against the followers of Allah's way) are looked upon with the same eye.

At-Tawhid in the Value System of Islam

So, Divine wisdom & justice demands that after this world in which the kafir (the infidel or the disbeliever) and the mu'min (the faithful or the believer), the lewd and the virtuous equally enjoy material blessings, there be another world (i.e., Ma'ad - the Resurrection) the blessings of which will be exclusively endowed to the faithful and Allah's friends and the torment of which will be exclusively given to the infidels and the enemies of Allah (SWT).

So, knowing the Almighty Allah and the attributes particular to Him creates these other beliefs, like the main root of the tree which when planted inside the earth, other roots will be brought into existence from it, which however, collectively form a system. When these roots become firm and the tree starts its vital activity, it begins to develop branches and leaves, namely, these beliefs affect man's action and give direction to his behavior, just as in the ideological system of Islam, At-Tawhid is the fundamental pivot and the mother root, so also in the value system of Islam, Al-Tawhid (monotheism, worshiping the One God - Allah) and serving Allah (SWT) is the essence of all values, and basically any value set forth in Islam traces back to worshiping Allah (SWT).

At-Tawhid - The Pivot of the Value System (of Islam)

Unlike other value systems, the value system is not constituted by dispersed and inharmonious elements, rather, it is an overall value which is manifested in various forms and which is regarded as miscellaneous manifestations of worshiping Allah (SWT). The root of these values in Islam is devoting one's heart to Allah (SWT) and whole-heartedly loving Him, and it is with the existence of this love that all values emerge and man no longer gets attached to this world. The one who falls in love with Allah (SWT) and firmly plants His love in his heart will no longer love the luxuries of this world and the worldly possessions will not be of any value to him.

If a man whose heart is to be Allah's place (as there is a riwayat which says: *"A mu'min's (a faithful person's heart) is the 'Arsh (the throne of Allah) of Allah, The Compassionate")* attaches his heart to worldly possessions such as cattle, land & stones, he has certainly not known Allah (SWT), for, if a person knows Allah (SWT), he will know that no one other than Him is worthy of being worshiped, then he will acquire no love for this world, and when there is no love for this world, there will no longer emerge any jealousy, envy, stinginess, enmity and rancor.

At-Tawhid in the Value System of Islam

There will no longer emerge so many evils and mischiefs which are the result of love for worldly position, there will no longer emerge oppressions and injustice stemming from domination-seeking and the root of all such conflicts, which arc due to the worldly matters, will dry up. To the one who has no love for worldly possessions, the existence and non-existence of such, possessions are the same. Such a person wants worldly possessions to be a means for his perfection, or to spend them in the way of Allah (SWT) so that it will be rewarded with a lasting reward (in the Hereafter) for him (by Allah (SWT)).

The one, who comes to know Allah (SWT) and in whose heart is Allah's love becomes established will want for Allah (SWT) each and every thing he may want. If Allah (SWT) commands him to hold such and such a position so that by holding that position he could serve the people, he will accept Allah's command whole-heartedly, hut if it is just a passion, he will never attempt to hold such a position, because it would become an idol and At-Tawhid is not consistent with worshiping idols.

There is a hadith (tradition) with various documents in our books on riwayat, including the book al-Kafi as follows:

At-Tawhid: Monotheism

> *"The ruin which two wolves, one from the front, and the other from behind, that causes a herd to be left alone by its herder, is not greater than a ruin caused to a Muslim's faith by love of wealth and love of position".*[4]

Imagine a herd of sheep left alone by its shepherd and this herd (without their shepherd) has been caught by two wolves having attacked the herd, from two sides. How much of these sheep do you think will remain unharmed? Obviously, no sheep will he left unharmed and a great harm will be suffered by the herd.

In the above hadith, the Holy Prophet (SA) of Islam says that the harm caused by two hungry wolves for a herd of sheep, is not more than the harm caused by love for wealth and position to a Muslim's faith, because the love of wealth and love of position become idols for persons and drive them out of At-Tawhid. So, just as At-Tawhid constitutes the root of all facts and the axis of an ideological system or in today's words, the pivot of the worldview of Islam, so it is also the pivot of the value system and the ideology of Islam.

---

[4] "Usul al-Kafi", vol. 2; p. 315, Hadith 2 and the translated text of Usul al-Kafi, vol. 4, p. 3.

At-Tawhid in the Value System of Islam

Can at-Tawhid be Found by Education?

Discussion about the issue of At-Tawhid has various dimensions, part of which is specialized and technical in nature and has to be surveyed in scientific centers, just as the reality of At-Tawhid and the knowledge of Allah (SWT) is a light which has to be shone by the Almighty Allah in fit and pure hearts and that reality will not be acquired through discussion and dialogue.

In the du'a (invocation to Allah) of 'Arafah by Sayyid'ush-Shuhada' (The Lord of the Martyrs) Al-Imam Al-Husain (AS), we read:

"O Allah! You are the One who shone the lights in the hearts of Your righteous servants so that they knew You and Your Oneness and You are the One who wiped out the aliens from the hearts of Your righteous servants so that they love none but You and took refuge in none but You." [5]

However, in spite of all this, it is not so that the discussion and education about the issues of At-Tawhid be closed and there be no way other than shining lights in the hearts, as the exalted Prophets (AS) too, taught realities concerning At-Tawhid alongside emphasizing action, Ikhlas (sincerity of intention) in the acts of worship, and would miss no

---

[5] "Mafatihul Jinan", the end of Du'a'u 'Arafah.

opportunity, even in the battle-field and during Jihad (Holy War) for the expansion of this great knowledge.

As already mentioned, At-Tawhid on one hand constitutes the pivot of the ideological system and the more it becomes perfect, the greater will become the belief in other realities and beliefs which are in fact manifestations of faith and belief in At-Tawhid and on the other hand, it (At-Tawhid) is the structure of the value system of Islam, namely, each true perfection and virtue is acquired in the light of At-Tawhid and stems from the root of At-Tawhid.

In other words, when At-Tawhid is manifested in action, it bears the fruit of morality and virtue and its effects in the eternal world will be (attaining) different degrees of the paradise. So, difference in the degrees of the Paradise and true perfections are in fact subject to the difference of the stage and degree of At-Tawhid of men.

At-Tawhid in Creation

One of the most simple and most easy way to understand degrees of At-Tawhid is At-Tawhid in creation, namely, that one believes that the world of being has been created by One Creator. This belief existed even among the polytheists. The Holy Qur'an quotes from the polytheists of Makah and the idolaters who were during the life-time of the Holy Prophet (SA) of Islam as having said that concerning their idols they did not believe in creation, rather, they regarded the idols as a means for drawing near to the One God and said:

"...We do not serve then except that they make us nearer to Allah... (39:3)."

The idolaters imagined that Allah The Almighty, has daughters named the angels (God forbid) and with this imagination, they made imaginary physical portraits for them and worshiped them so that the souls and lords of those idols would he pleased and as a result they would intercede with the One God (for the idolaters).

In another ayah, the Holy Qur'an says:

"And if you ask them who created the heavens and the earth, they will certainly say Allah... (31:25)."

So, the Polytheists of Makah did not deny Allah, rather they believed in gods lower than the level of the One God and worshiped them by making their idols. They believed that gods hold the power and a authority over the world and that the affairs of the world are managed according to their view, i.e., it is they who are effective in the revolution of the moon and the sun, in the emergence of the earthly phenomena and in men's felicity and adversity, that some were in charge of the management of the seas, some others had undertaken the responsibility for the land, that some had supervision over the affairs of the wars and some managed the affairs of the men.

Theses polytheists considered the world to have numerous directors and believed in Lords of the species. And this is the mailer against which the Holy Qur'an has contested most severely. And, the Holy Qur'an clarifies to the people that the same One Who is the Creator of the world is also the (One) Lord and the Manager or the world and that none can cause any effect or change in His creatures without His permission.

With this explanation, it becomes clear that in Islam mere belief in the Oneness of the Creator is not sufficient and that Islam does not consider those who have such beliefs to be monotheists and worshipers of Allah The One and Only, rather, At-Tawhid in Lordship (belief in One Lord) should also be added to belief in One Creator.

At-Tawhid in Rububiyyah (Lordship)

If we comprehend Allah's Lordship and properly understand its reality, we will see that its concept is

At-Tawhid in the Value System of Islam

very extensive and has many manifestations. As a whole, Lordship is divided into two pans: One lordship is takwini (pertaining to creation) and the other lordship is tashri'i (pertaining to Divines laws and religion).

Al-Tawhid pertaining to lordship in creation is to believe that management and running of the world in the realities of creation are in the hand of the Almighty Allah and to believe that the revolution of the moon and the sun, the emergence of the day and the night, men's life and death and the protection of the creatures and the world from destructive strikes and clashes is with Allah and it is He Who preserves the heavens and the earth.

"Surely Allah upholds the heavens and the earth lest they come to naught... (35:41)."

Just in the same way, the coming into being of every creature in any part of this spacious world, its growth, its death, its reproduction and or its emerging any sign(s) of being, are all under the management and will-power of Allah The Almighty and there is no phenomenon outside the sphere of the Lordship of the Almighty Allah. Breathing, speaking, listening, the movement of the wind, the growth of the plants, the movement of even a little leaf on the branches of a tree, the movement of an ant, and even a movement of a gnat are not outside Divine Lordship and no being in any part of the world can make the least movement without His permission in creation.

Therefore, there will no longer be any room for independently bringing about changes or affecting by angels and other creatures of Allah and any change or effect brought about by the creatures, it is under Allah's permission in creation and due to the power Allah has given them and they have no independence of their own in the fulfillment of an action and in applying that power.

That is to say, it is not that even if Allah does not will, a creature is able to fulfill an action, bring about a phenomenon and/or create a change in the world. Allah's will-power in creation is dominant over the whole world and everything lies under His will-power. Of course, this does not mean compulsion and is neither inconsistent with men's freewill, the description on which has been given in its own place.

Rububiyyah Pertaining to Divine Laws

Another part of Lordship contains men's freedom of will and choice. Among the creatures, Allah (SWT) has created in this natural world, there are groups of which the movements, effects and evolutions arc

At-Tawhid in the Value System of Islam

subject to the actions which they fulfill out of their own freewill and they are human beings. To reach his true perfection, man must move with his own freewill and choice, for, if a movement emerges in man out of compulsion, it will not be a human movement.

For instance, if a man is lifted with a crane from one place and taken to another place, it would be a mechanical movement, not a human movement. Also the growth of the body which is common to the plants, animals and men is a vegetal movement and the movement will in reality be human which stems from the origin of man's freewill and choice, even though the will-power is bestowed upon man by Allah and it is Allah Who provides the conditions for work, it is also Allah Who creates the matter and it is also Allah Who gives man the ability to act and the fact is that in each and every moment man needs Allah's creation and bestowal, but in spite of all this, the action which emerges from man is from the origin or his own freewill and choice and such an act is human. Now let us see how Allah's management is, regarding these acts which man fulfills out of his own freewill.

Allah's Rububiyyah demands that besides putting the origins of willpower, choice, the means and the toots of work at men's disposal, He also introduces to him the proper knowledge of the true and straight way, lets him know the good and the bad and issues and stipulates commands and laws for his individual and social life and this is the meaning or Lordship in divine legislation.

So, At-Tawhid in Lordship in creation demands that man believes that the management or the affairs or the world and or men in creational matters which are beyond his own willpower are attributed to Allah the Almighty, just as at-Tawhid in regard to Rububiyyah pertaining to Divine Laws demands that man gets the direction for life only from Allah, regards the right of law-giving to be only Allah's and considers no other being to have any independent right in giving laws.

That is to say, to him the law should be valid which has been legislated by Allah's permission and which is based on the legislative permission of the Almighty Allah, the very permission which Allah has given to the Holy Prophet (SA) and the Infallible Imams (SA) and this permission has been communicated through the nass (divine decree, explicit stipulation) of the Infallible Imams (SA), in a general way, to the qualified Fuqaha (Islamic Jurisprudents), the very thing in our society which is recognized as one of the pivots of religion, namely,

Wilayatul Faqih (the guardianship of the Islamic Jurisprudents).

So, the laws are valid to the monotheists (believers in At-Tawhid because they are eventually supported by and based upon the divine legislative permission given by Allah and if such base and support do not exist, no law will be valid to the monotheists and rather it will be considered a kind of shirk (polytheism)).

Quranic Ayah in Regard to Rububiyyah Pertaining to Creation

Lordship in creation has many parables and innumerable ayat of the Holy Qur'an denote its validity. For instance, wherever we encounter the word Rabb (Lord) in the Holy Qur'an, it points this fact:

"O men! worship your Lord Who created you and those before you, so that you may practice taqwa (2:21)."

You should worship the One Who is the Lord of you, of those who were before you and of all creatures.

"That is Allah, your Lord, the Creator of everything; there is no god but He; whence are you then turned away (40:62)."

Your Lord is only Allah, so which way are you are being taken and to which direction are you being deviated? Your direction should be towards Allah Who is your Lord. The sentence *"Al-hamdu lillahi Rabbil alamin"* (All praise is due to Allah-The Lord of the worlds) (Surah 1 of the Holy Qur'an) which each Muslim is duty-bound to repeat at least ten times each day (in wajib salawat) is an emphasis on this matter that every day we repeatedly take notice of the fact that the Lordship of the world of being, the possession of power, authority and control over the world, the management and running of the world are wholly and perfectly in the hands of the Almighty Allah.

The Position of Lordship in Divine Legislation and the Required Level of at-Tawhid

As for Lordship in Divine Legislation, we know that from the Islamic perspective and in accordance with the teachings which the Holy Our' an presents, the origin of deviation in belief and action is Iblis which is the same being who had been created before Hazrat Adam (AS) and had been engaged in worshiping Allah for many years. Amirul-Mu'mineen (The commander of the faithful) Al-Imam 'Ali (AS) says in "Nahjul- Balaghah":

At-Tawhid in the Value System of Islam

> *"Iblis worshiped Allah for six thousand years, while we do not know whether it was the years of this world or of the years of the hereafter"*[6]

Iblis worshiped Allah for six thousand years and yet it is not known whether these years have been of the years of this world each year of which is 365 days or of the years of the other world each day of which is one thousand years. Anyhow, for a very long period of time which is not quite imaginable for us, Iblis had existed and had been worshiping Allah (SWT), so that the angels had though that Iblis was of the angels and had given it a place in their own ranks. But Iblis had a two-sided nature (namely, like man, it had free will) and had to be tested so that the level of its At-Tawhid and knowledge of Allah (SWT) would emerge and it would become clear whether he had the necessary level of At-Tawhid or not.

The test of Iblis was realized through Hazrat Adam (AS), in the way that after the creation of Hazrat Adam (AS), Iblis was commanded (By Allah) to perform sajdah (prostration) to Adam (AS). But Iblis disobeyed this Divine command and because of this disobedience, it was driven away from the nearness to Allah and became the head of the inmates of hell and the rest of the inmates of hell will go to hell for following Iblis.

---

[6] "Nahjul-Balaghah" of Fayd, p. 779.

At-Tawhid: Monotheism

But why the one who has worshiped Allah (SWT) in His Oneness is driven away from His nearness for one opposition and one sin and reaches such a level of wretchedness which is unthinkable for us? What is the secret behind the fact that so much worship is ignored and Iblis falls so low because of just one sin?

The analysis which on the basis of Islamic outlook can be made on this matter is that the sin of Iblis stemmed from defect in its At-Tawhid, manifested itself in the form of a practical disobedience (to Allah) and caused its fall. Because in reality Iblis did not believe in whatever Allah (SWT) commands, His creatures should accept His command unquestionably, Iblis said;

"...I am better than he; You have created me out of fire, while him did you create out of dust (7:12)."

What is this command You are giving me, how should I prostrate to Adam while I am better than him? These words in fact arose from Iblis spirit of disbelief and unfaithfulness and were demonstrative of his inner and hidden kufr. The Holy Qur'an says:

"...And he was one of the disbelievers (2:34)"

Such disbelief existed in Iblis before, but it had not yet emerged and turned into the stage of action. Iblis did not have belief up to the required level of At-Tawhid and did not believe that the right to command order and inhabit unquestionably belongs exclusively to Allah (SWT) and whatever He commands has to be fulfilled: otherwise, Iblis believed in the One God and he also talked to Allah.

"...You have created me out of fire, while him did you create out of dust (7:12)."

Iblis even believed in Allah's Lordship in creation and in the Resurrection Day.

"...Respite me until the day when they are raised up (7:14)".

So, Iblis had neither any defect in the principle of belief in Allah's being the Creator, or in belief in Allah's Lordship in creation and nor in belief in ma'ad. But still he falls so much! Why? Because he does not believe in Allah's Lordship in Law-giving (Divine legislation) and docs not regard Allah's command to be obeyed unquestionably, unless Allah's command would be consistent with (Ibis's) own thought and desire.

There are many evidences proving that the Almighty Allah regards those ones as mushrik (polytheist) who consider the right of independent law-giving for themselves or for the others, , including the Jews and the Christians who thought their 'ulama' (religious scholars) and monks to be their Lords and who are reproached by Allah:

> *"They have taken their doctors of law and their monks for lords besides Allah (9:31)."*

In the riwayat, in the interpretation of this ayah of the Holy Qur'an, it has been said that they unquestionably obeyed the chiefs of the churches and the synagogues. That is, just as they considered it necessary to obey the commands of Allah's Book, so also they regarded it incumbent to obey the command of the council of the church and the command of the council of the synagogue, such as also today such things exist among various Christian groups that sometimes the council of the church decides and makes a law named religious law, and the Christians are obliged to regard it as divine and Christian law.

This is in reality the shirk in legislation (law-giving) and in lordship in legislation. A monotheist should consider the right of law-giving to be independently for the Almighty Allah and should consider valid only the law which is given in the light of Allah's legislative permission.

So, the required level of At-Tawhid in Islam. namely, the first level at which man is considered a muwahhid (monotheist) from the Islamic viewpoint is that man believes in the Oneness of the Creator, the Oneness of the Lord in (relation to) creation and the Oneness of the Lord in (relation to) law-giving. That is, man should believe that the Creator, The Lord, The Master, The Holder of power and control over the world and also the Genuine is One.

At-Tawhid in Ubudiyyah (Servitude) to Allah

After belief in the above matters, there comes the turn of At-Tawhid in Ma'abud (The Worshiped One). That is, besides all these, a muwahhid (monotheist) person should believe that no one but Allah (SWT) Who is the Absolute Lord and the Absolute Law-Giver is worthy of being worshiped. Belief in this matter, (At-Tawhid in Divinity and in Being Worshiped) is among the 'usul (Principles) of the religion of Islam but its external practice is rated among the furu' of the laws of the religion of Islam. Therefore, for a muwahhid, it is necessary to know the Creator, the Lord and the Planner of the World, the Chief Law- Giver and also the Only One Who is worthy of being worshiped to be Allah and all these have been summed up in the pure word:

"La ilaha illallah (There is no god but Allah)."

At-Tawhid: Monotheism

This word, besides denoting At-Tawhid in (Allah's) being the Creator, also guarantees the other stages of At-Tawhid and without these, the least of At-Tawhid from the Islamic viewpoint is not achieved. This stage aside, there are the perfection stages of At-Tawhid which stages man should gradually reach from the viewpoint of knowing Allah and put into practice from the viewpoint of action.

The important point which should be pointed out here is that if a person really believes in At-Tawhid in Allah's Lordship, namely, if he regards the management of the affairs of the world to be exclusively in the hands of Almighty Allah, he will certainly observe certain effects in his life, the first stage of which being his refusal to bow down in humiliation to any being (other than Allah), because when man believes that the power and control of the whole being is in the hands of Allah, there is no longer any reason for him to pay homage to anybody.

A man bows down and pays homage to the others when he considers them to be effective in an action and or runner of an action. But when one the management that the whole world is in the Hands of One God, he no longer pays homage to anybody (but Allah). The Muslims of the early period of Islam, by realizing this very fact that the term At-Tawhid

At-Tawhid in the Value System of Islam

includes such meaning, were built-up and in a short lime this knowledge about Allah and His virtues were manifested out of them and they achieved such great positions.

All have heard that when the armies of Islam reached Iran, the Iranians sent a commander of an army to speak to the armies of Islam to ask them what they wanted to say and what they wanted from them, money, position, land or, did they want something else?

The troops of Islam, the very persons who had been trained in the light of Islam for several years and had benefited from the Holy Qur'an, had reached such a high level of attitude, broad-mindedness, and magnanimity of spirit and endeavor, replied:

"We have not come to take any money from you or to occupy any land, rather we have come to liberate Allah's creatures from the yoke of slavery to you. Our aim is that human beings all over the world be liberated from slavery and servitude to persons like themselves who are also the creatures of Allah."[7]

Man should acquire such greatness and should not make himself humble or low before anyone other than Allah.

---

[7] Ibnul-'Athir, "Al-Kamilu Fittarikh", vol. 2, p. 462.

Manifestations in At-Tawhid in Ubudiyyah to Allah

The slogan of "Allahu Akbar" (Allah is the Great) which today prevails in the Islamic Republic of Iran and for which slogan, namely, the slogan of "Allahu Akbar", the world knows us, conveys this very meaning that greatness and magnanimity is exclusive to Allah and that man should only humble himself to Allah and to no one else unless Allah commands to respect others, as He has commanded us to respect our parents:

"And make yourself submissively gentle to them with compassion... (17:24)."

Such an expression of submissiveness is 'ibadah (servitude) to Allah and humbling before His infinite greatness and a muwahhid does so only at the command of Almighty Allah. And the same is also true of humbling before the Holy prophet (SA) and the Infallible Imams (AS).

"O you who believe! Be not forward in the presence of Allah and His Messenger... (49:1)."

Otherwise the person of the Holy Prophet (SA) and the Imams (AS), apart from their relation to Allah The Almighty and the respect in which Allah has held them, from the viewpoint of a muwahhid,

At-Tawhid in the Value System of Islam

should not in themselves be sanctified and before them one should not humble himself. This respect too in which the people hold the successors of the Imam (AS) and today for the esteemed leader of the Islamic Revolution is in fact servitude to Allah.

This respect is not out of family relations with him, nor is it because of greed for wealth or fear of punishment. This is a sentiment which stems from At- Tawhid, and since our people have acquired the love for Allah, they hold in greater respect anybody who is nearer to Allah and who endeavors more for the establishment of His rule and before such a person, they consider their lives of little values.

That some Sunni brother accuse the Shi'ahs and the other Muslims of shirk, it is out of the misunderstanding that has arisen from this very matter. They imagine that At- Tawhid in Allah's Lordship and in His being the Worshiped (One demand that man holds no other one in respect, because if one does so and/or for example kisses the grave of the Prophet (SA) or the Imams (AS), he will be a mushrik.

Such accusations are due to unawareness of the fact that this respect is in fact the respect for Allah and for divine positions. Were it not for Allah's command and were it not for the relation which

Allah's awliya' (friends) have towards Allah - The exalted, this could be considered a stage of shirk, but now that it is done in obedience to Allah's command and due to the relation of Allah's awliya' to Him, it is not only not the shirk, but is also the very At-Tawhid, It is Allah Who commands us to respect His Prophets (AS) and awliya' and it is also Allah Who says: If anybody wants his sin to be forgiven (by Allah), he should go to the door of the house of the Holy prophet (SA) of Islam.

"... And had they, when they were unjust to themselves, come to you and asked forgiveness of Allah and the Messenger had (also) asked forgiveness for them, they would have found Allah Oft-returning (to mercy), Merciful (4:64)."

Allah says that for the forgiveness of your sins you should refer to the Holy Prophet (SA) of Islam, he asks (Allah for) forgiveness for you and you yourselves ask (Allah for) forgiveness, then Allah will forgive your sins, At that time too, the munafiqun (the hypocrites) said: "We will ask forgiveness before Allah Himself, then why should we also go to the Prophet?" They refused to go to the Holy Prophet (SA) of Islam, to express their want to him, to appeal to him and to request him to act as intercessor with Allah for them.

This refusal brought about their nifaq (hypocrisy) and deprived them of Allah's favor and of the Holy Prophet (SA)'s asking Allah for forgiveness for them and it was because of this very disregard and hypocrisy that Allah said (to the Holy Prophet (SA)): "Even if you ask forgiveness for them seventy times, they will not be forgiven (by Allah);" "Why? Because they rendered arrogance and disobedience towards Allah's command and did not observe the respect which they should have paid towards the Holy Prophet (SA) of Islam. Since they disbelieved in Allah's blessing, they are no longer deserving of Allah's forgiveness, even if the Holy Prophet (SA) himself asks forgiveness for them:

"Ask forgiveness for them or do not ask forgiveness for them; even if you ask forgiveness for them seventy times, Allah will not forgive them... (9:80)."

So, those who out of arrogance, refuse to pay respect to the Holy Prophet (SA) of Islam and to Allah's awliya' and feel scorned to be humble before Allah's awliya', will not deserve Allah's Mercy. They are not only not muwahhidun, but have rather the worst kind of shirk, namely, the very kind of shirk which Iblis had, whereas, had they any shirk in Allah's being the Creator, this would not cause so much degradation for them.

If those who have recognized the One God and who know that all things in the world arc in His hands disobey His command and arc arrogant before Him, they are then worse than those who have not known Him and hence Iblis is worse than the idolaters, though he had recognized Allah and had also worshiped Him, So, the one who has recognized Allah, has understood His greatness and still disobeys Him, is more deserving of fall and torment than the one who has not yet acquired any recognition of Allah and has not known Him.

Therefore, it should not be wrongly imagined that belief in At-Tawhid in Allah's Lordship has any inconsistency with the belief of the Shi'ahs and of the majority of the Muslims about the Prophets (AS) and the Holy Imams (AS).

We do not regard anyone to be independently effective in the creation and management of the world besides Allah and alongside Him, However, we believe that Allah The Almighty has granted certain powers to some of His creatures and that He has willed that many of the works he fulfilled through the channel of their will-power, Allah fulfills miracles at the hands of His Prophets (AS) and even that He revives the dead at the hands of 'Isa (Jesus Christ) (AS), it is by no means inconsistent with At-Tawhid in revival.

The true Reviver is Allah and it is He Who grants such a power to 'Isa (AS), the son of Maryam (AS) and also grants any power to anybody He wills, as He has willed to grant such power to our Holy Imams (AS) and this belief has not only no inconsistency with At-Tawhid, but is also of the stages of At-Tawhid. Just as Allah tested Iblis through commanding him to obey Adam (AS) and be humble before him, so He will also test other creatures of His through commanding them to obey His Prophets (AS) and awliya'.

"And We did not send any Messenger but that he should be obeyed by Allah's permission... (4:64)."

Thus, as Allah has commanded, it is incumbent upon all the people to obey the Prophets (AS) and the one who refuses to obey the Prophets (AS) has refused to obey Allah.

According to a riwayat, Iblis said to Allah: *"I will worship you as much as you want, exempt me from prostrating to Adam."* But Allah addressed him; *"If you want to worship Me, worship Me the way I want you to."* Otherwise, you have obeyed your own desire and worshiped your own passions. If you are a worshiper of Allah, you should step in the way which Allah has ordained, not the way which your own imperfect mind thinks, as some groups had invented some ways for worshiping Allah.

This kind of worship in fact traces back to worshiping oneself, not to worshiping Allah. Therefore, to believe that Allah's awliya' are endowed with certain levels of creational guardianship and bring about certain changes in this world by Allah's permission is the same as At-Tawhid and to appeal to them and to ask them for intercession (with Allah) has no sort of inconsistency with At-Tawhid.

The Reality of At-Tawhid

In this part of the discussion, it is very appropriate to take certain points. The first point is that: At-Tawhid is not just to profess by tongue and to bear witness to the Oneness of (Allah) and the Prophethood (of Prophet Muhammad (SA)) although the utterance of shahadatayn (the two witnesses by a Muslim that Allah (SWT) is One and Prophet Muhammad (SA) is His Messenger) cause a number of external decrees in this world to embrace the one (who utters the shahadatayn).

However, that At-Tawhid which is the source of man's eternal felicity and his true perfection docs not revolve around the axis of word and tongue, rather it (At-Tawhid) is a reality in the heart and is a faith which develops in the heart. To express At-Tawhid and to utter shahadatayn is a factor for which the person (who expresses At-Tawhid and utters the shahadatayn) receives Islamic treatment, his body is regarded as tahir (Islamically pure), he may marry a Muslim and his life and property is safe, and slaughtering of animals by him for meat is halal (Islamically lawful).

But it is by no means indicative of the perfection of the soul and eternal felicity (of the person), because there may be some who apparently claim Islam, whose life and property arc protected and the (meat of) an animal slaughtered by them is considered halal, but who have, however, no trace of spirituality and eternal salvation, and who even in the hereafter, are placed in the lowest parts of Hell, such as a munafiqun who apparently claim Islam, but who have no faith in their hearts, about whom the Holy Qur'an says:

"...the hypocrites are in the lowest stage of the fire... (4:145)."

And for this very reason in the hereafter, the condition of the hypocrites is worse than that of those who openly expressed kufr and shirk.

At-Tawhid: Monotheism

So, what becomes the source or eternal felicity is the faith in the heart which should develop in the heart out or insight and awareness and a muwahhid should devote his heart to Allah (SWT).

Expression of At-Tawhid With the Tongue and Not Out of Conviction

During the early period of Islam, there were some people who out of unawareness and following the social wave expressed about embracing Islam, in the way that when the distinguished classes of the society and the famous persons in the community became Muslim, then following them, this unaware class, too, embraced Islam. The Holy Qur'an, while accepting their external Islam and not rejecting them, warns them not to think that they have real faith, and tells them rather what they have acquired is an external Islam and that they should try so that iman (faith in Islam) enters into their hearts.

"The dwellers of the desert say: we believe. Say: You do not believe but say, we submit; ... (49:14)."

The desert-dwelling Arabs said that we believe and are like other believers. Allah The Almighty told the Holy Prophet (SA) of Islam to tell them that they have not yet believed and faith has not yet entered into their hearts, that however they were Muslims and if they wanted to become true believers and to use the spiritual and eternal effects of faith, they should try so that faith would enter into their hearts and that they would attain trust and certainty (in faith) and devote their hearts to Allah out of insight and awareness and that it is then that they would be among true believers.

Anyhow, one of the critical and dangerous currents of the early period of Islam was this very issue or nifaq, that a number of persons apparently expressed Islam, but did not believe in Allah and in the Holy Prophet (SA) in their hearts. Of course, shirk, and kufr have stages, just as Islam and iman have stages. Some of these munafiqun were the most obstinate enemies of Islam and of Prophet Muhammad (SA), but some others were not as obstinate although they did not like the Islamic system either. In description of some of these munafiqun the Holy Qur'an says:

"... And when they stand up for the salat they stand up sluggishly; they do it only to be seen of by the people and they do not remember Allah but a little (4:142)."

Such munafiqun take part in the salawat, go to the mosque, attend the congregational prayers, but with listlessness, languidness, without enthusiasm and just for showing themselves to the others and making them believe that they are also among those who recite salawat; and by attending religious gatherings their purpose is also the same, as the Holy Qur'an says:

"...They do it only to be seen of by the people and they do not remember Allah but a little (4:142)."

And in their hearts they have but little remembrance of Allah and this is one of the styles of the Holy Qur'an that if some individuals have even a little attention to and remembrance (of Allah), Allah makes an exception of them.

By the above statements we meant to point out the fact that external Islam may be accompanied by inner disbelief; there may be persons who are apparently Muslims and who even perform the acts of the Muslims, but who have no faith in their hearts, for iman is a different matter. That it is said that the body of a person who has uttered shahadatayn is tahir and his blood is immune, should not prompt one to imagine that eternal felicity is also attained by him. The former is one matter and the latter is another matter. The former concerns fiqh (Islamic Jurisprudence) and the latter concerns beliefs and commandments.

Obligation to at-Tawhid

Another point which should be taken note of is that some feeble-minded persons who more or less exist in all societies, when coming across the mutashabih (metaphorical, intricate) Ayat and riwayat, mean them according to their own advantage and do not pursue the muhkam (clear) Ayat and riwayat which interpret the mutashabih ayat. For instance, there is a riwayat which states; *"If anybody utters the word 'La ilaha illallah' (There is no god but Allah), he will enter Paradise"*.

There is also the well-known silsilatudh-e-dhahab (The golden chain) riwayat from Al-Imam 'Ali ibn Musa Ar-Rida (AS) (the eighth Imam of the Shi'ahs) which states: "The words la ilaha illallah are my fortress." The weak-minded individuals think that just saying "La iaiha illallah" suffices to make one enter Paradise, whereas mere verbal utterance and the movement of the tongue do not work and can only be the source of external decrees. In the terminology of Ayat and riwayat, by uttering a word, verbal utterance is not meant, rather belief in the heart is meant which has been interpreted in other riwayat and reference should be made to them, so that by paying attention to those interpreting and muhkam riwayat, the meaning of such mutushabihat and intricate ayat and riwayat be realized. Or in the Holy Qur'an we read:

At-Tawhid: Monotheism

> *"Surely Allah does not forgive that anything should be associated with Him, and forgives what is besides that to whomsoever He wills... (4:48)."*

Some persons infer from such kind of Ayat that the rest of the sins are not important and it is enough for a person just to avoid saying God is two to enter Paradise and Allah forgives the rest of the sins, as the Holy Qur'an says:

> *"... And forgives what is besides that to whomsoever He wills... (4:48)."*

Such superficially derived inferences which stem from ignorance and the spirit of slackness, should not become the source of our deception and we should not let ourselves he deceived by Satan by this means. The matter is not so simple.

The Meaning of the Term At-Tawhid and the Initiation of Distortion in It

To clarify the matter, we should better give the meaning of the term At-Tawhid and take advantage of the ayat and the riwayat for the interpretation of this significant Islamic Principle which is the root of all beliefs and values.

The term At-Tawhid means to regard as one and only. However, in the common usage of Islam and

At-Tawhid in the Value System of Islam

according to Religious Jurists it means to regard Allah as one and only and does not mean to regard everything as one and only. Some leftist deviated groups try to mean At-Tawhid in such a way as to be consistent with their own vested interests.

They say At-Tawhid means to make one and since it is not possible to make Allah one, because Allah is Himself One, so At-Tawhid has nothing to do with the Oneness of Allah and by At-Tawhid it is meant that the society should be made one; class differences should be removed so that a new society with oneness be created. These arc the so-called Islamic Marxist groups who had been impressed by the Marxist school of thought and wanted to give Islamic color to their own Marxist ideology.

We know that Marxism in the philosophy of history and historical materialism propounds that human society is moving towards a classless society, in the way that the differences existing in the society will intensify and reach to an extent where class differences will totally be removed and all people will be the same as far as enjoying the offerings of the material life is concerned. In other words, the people will reach a new balanced society.

These leftist groups , too, molded the same expression with "Tawhidi (based on Tawhid- related

At-Tawhid: Monotheism

to Tawhid) suffix and said: "a new balanced Tawhidi society" and by Tawhid they meant the very unity of class or removal of classes, and for proving it they reasoned that basically Tawhid means *"to make one"* and this has nothing to do with God.

These mixed and in fact atheistic thoughts left ill-effects upon our unaware youth so much so that it became one of the greatest dangers for Islam and the Muslims.

As for the term "Tawhid", which is from the infinitive "taf'il" in Arabic literature, sometimes it is employed to mean *"making one"* and sometimes to mean *"considering one"* and we know that the infinitive "taf'il" is not always employed for making transitive of its famous meaning. There are many words which we even employ in our Persian expressions, which words though are of the infinitive "taf'il", yet do not have that meaning.

For example, the words "ta'zim", "takfir", "tamjid", "tasbih", "taqdis", "takrim" and the like which are all of the infinitive "taf'il", yet none of which mean La bring about the quality. You have heard that it is said that for such and such a person "takfir" is made. By saying this word, is kufr infidelity, disbelief created in him? Or, is he regarded as "kafir" (infidel, disbeliever), or, when for a witness is declared "tafsiq" in a law-court, and it is said that "this witness is a fasiq (an evil-doer) and thus his appearing as a witness is not acceptable."

Is fisq (evil-doing) created in him? Or, is he considered as a fasiq (an evil-doer)? When it is said that for such and such a person was offered ta'zim, is it meant that 'azamah (greatness- the adjective of the infinitive ta'zim) has been created in him (by those who offer to him ta'zim)? All of you pay ta'zim (respect) to Imam. Do you (by so doing) create 'azamah (greatness) in him or do you perceive his 'azamah (greatness)? All of us utter takbir for Allah (to pronounce Allah's glory through the call "Allahu Akbar" (Allah is the greatest). Do we (by doing so) create greatness in Allah (SWT) or consider Him as great and recall His greatness?

These are all from the infinitive taf'il At-Tawhid too means to regard Allah (SWT) as One, not to make Him or any other thing one. Even if we have a classless society in Islam and it is also desirable, it does not concern as At-Tawhid as a principle of faith of Islam, and it is interesting to note that in the Holy Qur'an, the word At-Tawhid and its derivatives are not found at all and this great Islamic principle has appeared in the Holy Qur'an in other wordings. The Holy Qur'an says:

At-Tawhid: Monotheism

> *"And your God is one God! There is no god but He... (2:163)."*

Your God is One and Only God and He has no partner, either inside or outside His Being.

The discussion is about knowing Allah, not the society, so the creation or non-creation of oneness of class cannot be meant here.

Anyhow, this was one of the greatest intellectual distortions which were made towards this ideological principle of Islam, and sometimes it was even said: "Basically God in Islam is a moral concept and is not propounded as a true and real being." Sometimes it was said: "God and the hereafter do not have philosophical concept, rather utter goodness, absolute perfection, forgoing worldly pleasures and profits and in one word moral ideal is the very God and He has no external existence either (God forbid) and that we should pursue these absolute words and try to become perfect and that worshiping God means just this."

Wrong Imaginations Concerning the Meaning of At-Tawhid

Some others believed that just giving the world a movement by Allah and so to say His giving the world a start suffices for the world wheel to rotate

At-Tawhid in the Value System of Islam

till eternity, without being in any need of Allah again. Such a way of thinking existed even among some philosophers and probably that some philosophers of the ancient Greece called God as the first stimulant has stemmed from this very thought. Some groups or Islamic philosophers have also had such inclinations arid it is regrettable that such a deviational way or thinking has been from those who also believed in the Only Allah, let alone the atheists and the polytheists.

Such way of thinking, namely, to think that Allah's work is just the creation of this world, or at most inflicting the first blow or the primary stimulation, is totally rejected in Islam.

Allah (SWT) introduced by Islam is the One Who is constantly planning the world matters and Who if does not will the survival of the world for even a single moment, everything will he destroyed and the very non-will of Allah for the survival of the world suffices for the world to be destroyed and in such a case, there is no need for Allah to destroy the world, like a builder who takes a pick and destroys a building. The destruction of the world does not need such a process.

Although, with our imperfect minds, we cannot realize the true relation of Allah and the world, but for approximation to the mind, it can be said that the mental images which are created in the mind, the scene of a garden, a battlefield and or other things arc created by the mind and despite their being existing in the mind and their being capable of creating certain effects,[8] yet their survival is subject to Allah's attention and His will and if Allah's will and his attention is removed from them, there will no longer he left anything.

The God introduced by Islam is such a God upon Whose will depends the whole world or being and Who if wishes something to come into existence, it will come into existence and if wills the destruction of something, that thing will he destroyed. The emphasis of the Holy Qur'an, too, is in the first place, on the concept of Rabb (The Lord), i.e., we should know Allah as Rabb (The Lord), The slogan of Islam is not *"there is no creator but Allah"*, so to think that the world only needs creation and from then on, namely, after being created it will stand on its own, is not an Islamic thought.

Some, too, had imagined that the meaning of "Allah plans the world" is that a pre-made plan has been fulfilled in the past hundreds and thousands of

---

[8] Sometimes mental imaginations have certain effects, for example, if one imagines sour things, his mouth waters and/or on imagining pleasing or displeasing things, one feels pleasure or displeasure and on the whole, the renewal of memories have effects.

years, in the way that Allah, has, for example, drawn a map and arranged the world factors according to that map and has no longer any concern for and attention to the world, and has nothing to do with the world affairs. This was the belief held by some Jews. They said: *"God has created the world and should also plan it, but not (plan it) always, rather, in the beginning of creation, God has made a plan, drawn a map and implemented it on the world and does not interfere in the world affairs any longer."*

The Holy Qur'an quotes them as saying:

"And the Jews say: Allah's hand is tied up! May their hands be tied and they be cursed for what they said. Nay, both His hands are stretched out... (5:64)."

They thought that God has implemented a plan/map and that His hands are then tied up, like an engineer who draws the map of a building, implements and constructs it and when it has been constructed, the engineer can no longer change it, (they thought) that God, too, had a plan for the world, implemented it in the world and it will continue to be implemented forever and it cannot be changed any longer (God forbid).

These beliefs of the Jews in matters of creation and religious legislations had some manifestations. On the one hand, they say that since the planning of the world is unchangeable, so praying and appealing are of no use and do not solve any problem. On the other hand, they believed that the system of religious law which God has ordained for the world and which is also not changeable, is the very system Prophet Musa (Moses) (AS) has brought from the Almighty Allah as tablets and that since God's will has rested upon these decrees and it is unchangeable, so abrogation in decrees does not exist either. Such a thought is not acceptable in the viewpoint of Islam. The Holy Qur'an says:

"...Every moment He is in a state (of glory) (55:29)."

According to the Holy Qur'an, Allah is planning the world the everyday and every moment, and any moment He wills, He can change the plans of the world and nothing has and will come outside His powerful hands and all things are in His hands. No force affects Him and no factor ties up His hands.

Of course it should be noted that there are also immutable divine destinations and immutable divine decrees, but this does not mean that we should think that the world system is a compulsory system, that man has no right in it, and that prayers, appealing (to Allah), reliance on Allah, endeavors, efforts and jihad (endeavoring in the way of Allah) cannot change pre-destinations. There are changeable pre-destinations which are changed with jihad.

The Subject of Bada'

Here, it is useful to also point out about the subject of bada' (the belief that Allah (SWT) can change the world affairs at any moment). To believe that at any moment Allah can change the trends of the world, nullify the past factors, create more powerful factors in their place, is termed as bada' in the terminology of Islamic learning. There is a riwayat as follows:

"No 'ibadah (Allah's worship) is superior to belief in Bada"[9], that is, the same belief which is set forth in the face of people like the Jews and due to which one (having such belief) notices that in any situation, Allah is able to change the causes and requirements and bring about new conditions. This belief, on one hand, makes one hopeful of the future, so that even if apparent causes are not at hand, he will not despair and lose hope and on the other hand makes him fearful about his own future, and this is the very thing which is desirable in the value system or Islam.

That is to say, man should always be in a state between fear and hopefulness, so that he will fully

---

[9] "Al-'Usul al-Kafi", vol. 1, p. 46, Hadith 1 and the translated text of "Al-'Usul al-Kafi", vol. 1, p. 200.

realize his need of Allah (his being invariably in need of Allah) and so, if a misfortune befalls him, he will not think that this misfortune is lasting and that it will not be removed. If there is a misfortune (facing him), he should be hopeful of its removal, in the way that he should start struggling and making efforts and also beseech Allah so his problem will he solved. If he has a material and worldly blessing, he should not become proud and gay and should not think that (his blessing is ever-lasting and that he will never lose it.

Even for the survival of his spiritual blessings, man should constantly be stretching his hands (for begging) to Allah and should beseech Allah to make those blessings lasting for him} For instance, this very Islamic Republic system is one of the greatest gifts and blessings Allah has granted us. If we know the value of this blessing and are thankful for it, it will continue, otherwise there is no guarantee for its survival.

Clarification of Mechanical and Dynamic Movements

Earlier it has been mentioned that some Western scientists have imagined that God has just inflicted a stimulating force on the world and that He has no longer anything to do with it and that the world itself with this movement and transference of power becomes the cause of other movements and developments in the world of matters and gradually brings the phenomena into existence.

Some others have imagined the movement of the world of nature to be dynamic, that is, if in the above mentioned way of thinking, God was thought of as the Creator of power in the world of nature, in this way of thinking only the existence of the nature is attributed to Allah (SWT) and the developments of the world are attributed to the dynamic movement of the matter itself.

These individuals had in fact accepted the same view of dialectic materialism and considered the developments of the world to be dynamic developments and just for having an Islamic color, they said: *"The essence of the matter has been created by God, but He no longer has any role in it and the developments of the matter and the emergence of new and new phenomena are as a result of the dynamic movement of the nature itself, and it is the world which through its natural movement gradually brings about changes and creates phenomena. The phenomena of life, too, gradually come into existence in the world and evolve into various animals till they reach man."* (Just as the so-called 'theory of evolution' is illustrated.).

At-Tawhid: Monotheism

Between this way of thinking and the Islamic view there is a difference of 180 degrees. The Holy Qur'an teaches us that then Almighty Allah is continuously involved in creation and that no being, in any moment is needless of Allah.

To reject the above view (dynamic movement), we start with the most simple reasons which are understandable, perceivable and absorbable and with a simple expression which does not need accurate philosophical foundations either, we say that dynamic movement, supposing that it exists in the essence of the nature and is clarifiable and acceptable in a way, can never cause the emergence of a new being, because, just as mechanical movement is nothing hut the transference of an object from one place to the other, dynamic movement is also nothing more than the natural development of the matter itself and can never create a new being which is not of the category of matter and the materials and which has not been in the matter before, either, though it can create developments in the lifeless matter.

We constantly see that living beings come into existence in the world, possessed of intelligence, senses, emotions (and in the case of man) possessed of initiative, free-will, creativity, qualities which cannot he attributed to the matter, and even the materialists themselves admit this reality that intelligence and will- power is not a material matter and do not have the quality of the matter, but to justify their view, they say: *"These are brought into existence by themselves and as a result of the developments of the matter"*- a view which means the emergence of a being without a cause and without a creator,

Anyhow, it is obvious that natural movement, whether it be thought of in the mechanical form (namely, as a result of the force which enters the object from outside) or in the dynamic form (which is the natural requisite of the matter itself and the matter is naturally mobile and dynamic) does not create soul and life, intelligence and will-power do not come into existence from it.

So, the emergence of living phenomena, both animal and man which is taking place in this world continuously indicates that a creator is continuously giving life to these creatures and creates them and that not just once, but in various stages. For instance, man, though has one soul, he does not have one creation. The Holy Qur'an says:

"...He creates you in the womb of your mothers-a creation after a creation... (39:6)."

From the moment human sperm enters (a mother's) womb, creations start, when it turns into 'alaqah (clot), it acquires a new share of life which it has not had before. This (being given the) share of existence requires a creator, because the sperm itself does not possess the perfections of 'alaqah, nor can it create those perfections. These perfections have been granted to it by the Creator. The Holy Qur'an says:

"Then We made the life-germ a clot, then We made the clot a lump of flesh, then We made (in) the lump of flesh bones, then We clothed the bones with flesh, then We caused if to grow into another creation ... (23:14)."

Each development it acquires, and each new share of existence it gets, is a new creation which has to be granted by Allah (to it). The creation of the essence of the matter is not sufficient for the creation of these new perfections of existence which are being realized anew and this makes no difference with regard to man, animals and the plants.

A plant-seed, when placed inside the earth, absorbs water, is soaked, and physical and chemical effects are developed in it. But when the seed starts growing, stretches a root inside the earth and sends a stem out of the ground, it has acquired new shares of life and existence which it did not have before.

At-Tawhid in the Value System of Islam

These effects do not exist in a dead seed, nor can dynamic movement create this plant movement. Then it grows, turns into a stem and bears branches and leaves. These, too, have a new life and a fresh share of existence.

The same holds true of flowers, blossoms, beautiful and startling colors, pleasant smells; by the time the fruit appears, each have a new creation which is fulfilled by the Creator. To move further, even the beings in whom new developments are not observed and who arc thought of as having a monotonous existence, has to receive their existence from the Creator at any moment.

So, in general, the beings at each and every moment need to be granted life by the Almighty Allah. We, who arc seated or standing here now, do not have our tomorrow's life and existence. We may be destroyed and so there would be no tomorrow for us. So the tomorrow's existence does not exist now and a Creator will create it tomorrow. Tomorrow may be too far (for our discussion): Let's consider the next hour.

We do not own, nor have the existence of the next hour. When the next hour comes, Allah will grant us that existence. Let us also set aside the next hour and consider the next minute, We do not own our

At-Tawhid: Monotheism

own life in the next minute, it is also in Allah's hands. If He wills, He will grant us this existence and if He does not will, our life will not continue.

If we acquire such knowledge about Allah The Almighty, it is then that we can accept, admit and believe in Allah's hand in all existence and in all conditions. But that view which says: 'God created the matter, but then it is the automatic movement of the matter which becomes the source of the emergence of beings', will never acquire such knowledge (of God). Those who hold such a view, regard themselves as having been left to themselves in the world, neither realizing any need to God, nor expecting any help from Him.

In their view, God created a matter which is automatically moving, or/and that according to mechanical imagination, God inflicted the primary movement upon this world and has no more anything to do with it, like a clock which a skillful clock-maker makes and tunes in such a way that its tune continues to exist for ever and does not need to be tuned anew.

Usually, when clocks are tuned, after a while, due to the gradual consumption of the mechanical energy, they come to need tuning anew. But if the system is arranged so that this energy which remains inside

At-Tawhid in the Value System of Islam

the clock is not consumed, is again transferred to the spring and causes the movement of the hands of the clock to continue till eternity, there will no longer be any need for the clock-maker and the tuner.

Some have thought of the world current this way and imagined that God has tuned and then set aside the world.

Another group says that the world did not even need the primary tuning either, that this is the inherent movement of the nature which automatically emerges in it and proceeds to any place the causes and conditions might demand. These are not Islamic views. These arc the modern forms of shirk.

In the view of Islam, the existence of the world is in Allah's hands at each and every moment successively and ceaselessly, each being, with whatever share of existence it may he endowed and whatever sign of existence it may acquire, receives it from Allah (SWT) and is in need of Him, so that if He does not will the existence or the world for even a single moment, the whole world will be brought to naught. In the Islamic way of thinking, no power other than the power of Almighty Allah governs the world of being.

At-Tawhid: Monotheism

The other powers are a limited ray of His infinite power, are dominated by Him and are effective just in the extent He has granted permission in creation for their effectiveness.

> "...And (He created) the sun and the moon and the stars, made subservient by His command; surely His is the creation and the command; blessed is Allah, the Lord of the worlds (7:54)."

The movement of the moon and the stars, the shining of the sun, the growth of each plant, the splitting or even a single seed, and/or a sick man's being healed are all with the will of Allah and subdued by His Will-Power. If Allah does not will, no being can do anything.

The holders of such (an Islamic) view, attach no value to any power (other than Allah's) and let no fear enter their hearts in the face of the threats of the enemies of Islam, because they know that wherever any power exists, it is dominated by Allah's Will-power.

> "...Allah is the Master of His affair... (12:21)."

It is such spirit that makes the Muslim combatant at the front or jihad so strong that he fears nothing, because he knows that:

At-Tawhid in the Value System of Islam

> *"If Allah assists you, then there is none that can overcome you, and if He forsakes you, who is there then that can assist you after Him... (3:160)."*

Those who have been raised with such a culture, bow their heads to no power (other than Allah), to them everything is humble and worthless and to them is valuable only that which has a way to Allah and which is related to the source of power, greatness and glory, (i.e., Allah), as the Holy Qur'an says:

> *"...And to Allah belongs the might and to His Messenger and to the believers... (63:8)."*

Glory and honor is for Allah, His messengers and the believers and the others are all abject and humiliated. If there is glory, it is that which Allah has granted and He has ordained this degree, in the first place for the exalted position of the Holy Prophet of Islam, Muhammad al-Mustafa (SA) and after him, to the extent any person who is closer to Allah (SWT), whose faith is greater and whose relation to Him is firmer, enjoys such a glory.

It is with the Islamic view that a Muslim views all the forces of the nature as nothing before the infinite divine Power and feels such glory and greatness inside himself which make him invincible.

He knows that power is not just these material powers, though these very material powers are also created by Allah and the power over them lies in Allah's hands, rather the supernatural powers and the divine aids are also in Allah's hand. Where He wills, the water of the Nile River drowns Fir'awn (Pharaoh) and his men in it and where He wills, one divine cry from the heavens destroys and vanishes a people.

Therefore, At-Tawhid in creation demands that one believes that each creature in any condition, any place and at any time is in need of Allah and will never be needless of Him.

Divine Management

The next stage is the stage of Rububiyyah. In this stage, one should not only believe that creation is from Allah, but should rather believe that the developments of the matter, and the relation of creatures with each other, the effects they make and the effects made upon them are all under Allah's management and command.

Here, again two extreme inclinations exist: some, when faced with these expressions (related to At-Tawhid) of the Holy Qur'an, imagined that the meaning of at-Tawhid in creation and in Lordship is that no other creature has any effect of its own (as is

At-Tawhid in the Value System of Islam

observed in the Asha'irah (Ash'arite school of thought) and these materially affecting and being affected is just a superficial relationship or as some say: "God's habit has ordained that when fire falls on a piece of wood, it burns, otherwise there is no relation between them."

Though their goal and motive or making such remarks has been to reach the ultimate degree of At-Tawhid, but they have neglected the fact that Allah The Almighty is not incapable of giving an effect to its creature. It is true that the essence of being is from Allah and each creature in any moment receives its being, its existence from Him, but this does not mean that no being has any effect.

If it meant so, then the system of divine legislation would he a meaningless system, If the words you speak, the voice you hear, the decision you take, the work you do, the acts of worship you fulfill and the jihad you embark upon were not the effects of your being, and you had no role in their creation, then in this case there would be no difference between the obedient and the disobedient, since (according to the above supposition) Allah (SWT) had created one obedient and the other disobedient.

So, why should He reward the former and punish the latter? The impression of causes and reasons on the emergence or effects is not deniable. However, the fact to be emphasized is that these are all subordinate to a higher power, that it is He Who constantly grants them the grace of existence and endows them the signs of existence and renders them effective with His own permission. Let us consider a statement of the Holy Qur'an in this regard. It says:

> "...And when you determined out of clay a thing like the form of a bird by My permission... (5:110)".

In the above Ayah, the Almighty Allah addressing; 'Isa (AS) (Jesus Christ), the son of Maryam (AS), says that he brings into existence, but with His (Allah's) will and that he heals (the blind and the leper) but with His (Allah's) will. That is to say, the authority and the will has not come outside Allah's hand, This is the light of existence which emanates from Allah, but at the hands of Ibrahim (AS) (Prophet Abraham), Isma'il (AS) (Prophet Ishmael), 'Isa (AS) or Musa (AS) (Prophet Moses), or any other of Allah's Prophets (AS) and awliya', and through the channel of their will-power, choice and option. The whole matter lies just here.

To totally deny the impression of causes, would be to believe that the world is based on fatalism, leaving no room for duty, all learning's should be

At-Tawhid in the Value System of Islam

washed away, because (according to such assumptions) they no longer have any relation to each other, no cause affects any effect, no microbe has any role in the emergence of sickness and no medicine cures any ailment, But this is not the case. Allah has put this effect in the medicine and the medicine falls effective with Allah's permission, and this matter makes no difference whether in natural matters and/or in supernatural matters and the Prophet who heals a sick man also does so with Allah's permission. Those who have not been able to understand the combination between these two imagine that if we say that a Prophet, an Imam or one of Allah's friends has healed a sick person, this will become shirk.

Anyhow, Allah may grant a power to His wali (friend) to revive a sick person by His permission or to manifest other miracles and wonderful workings. But those who have thoughts that the man is compelled to do everything and has no option, by attributing actions and effects to Allah in a direct manner, arc considerable preys for the colonialists, the oppressors and the tyrants, as in the lime of the Omayyad's and the Abbasids, under the pretext of strengthening the spirit or At-Tawhid, they more or less spread these thoughts that the man is compelled and not free, thereby creating weakness in the people, while these two facts should be understood together, combined together, and attain the great effect resulting from them.

Both the spirit of At-Tawhid should be completely strengthened, namely, no independent power exists but that of the Almighty Allah and also the effect of causes and particularly the effect of man in his optional acts should be taken into consideration and it should be known that the basis of religions is the recognition of free-will. If there had been no free-will, then no room would be left for teaching, guidance, revelation of Books, sending of Prophets, warning and giving of good tidings (by Allah). The Prophets warn the people against Allah's torment which befalls them due to their bad actions, whereas if there were compulsions (as fatalists hold) then no room would be left for fear and torment.

Divine Wilayah

With these introductory statements we conclude that not only the planning of the whole world as a total system is in Allah's hand, but also every trivial system and every small system has also its own plan which is fulfilled under Allah's Will-power. In the midst of all these, man's plan, because of his miscellaneous virtues and aptitudes, has very extensive and widespread dimensions each or which necessitates a particular plan (or management). That pan of divine plan which concerns sense- possessing

At-Tawhid in the Value System of Islam

creatures including man is in the language of the Holy Qur'an, called wilayah.

In the Holy Qur'an, we come across ayat in which the words wali (Islamic jurisprudential guardian), wali (governor, ruler) and Mawla (master) have been employed and mentioned as names and attributes for Almighty Allah. All these have been derived from the root wilayah which briefly includes the meaning of taking charge or and managing the affairs of the sense-possessing beings.

That is, the Almighty Allah, after creating man, does not leave him to himself. Rather, He has undertaken the planning of his life and arranges the events so that he can go ahead in the direction of perfection and growth. (That we say: "he can go ahead in the direction of perfection" is because man is a free agent, possessed of free-will and in spite of the existence of all conditions and facilities, he can still misuse the same and traverse the way of fall and decline instead of following the way of perfection and exaltation.).

However, Allah's work in this field is fulfilled in two dimensions or in two stages; one pertains to AI-Wilayatul-ammah (general guardianship) towards all men and the other pertains to Al-wilayatul- khassah (particular guardianship). The Almighty Allah in all periods of history and in all pans at the world has laws and traditions which provide the grounds for the growth and perfection of all men. This is a general guardianship which is implemented towards all men, whether some people accept this guardianship and submit themselves to the position of divine guardianship, or they indulge in kufr and rebellion (against Allah's commands). Anyhow, this true divine guardianship exists towards the faithful and the infidel, the pious and the impious and will become manifest on the Resurrection Day.

"Here is protection only Allah's, the True One... (18:44)."

It is then that divine guardianship becomes manifest and it becomes known that His wise management has been and is governing over the whole world.

But the Holy Qur'an, in many cases, has also talked about particular guardianship which is only for the mu'minin and the muwahhidun, namely, those who make good use of these grounds and have attempted to achieve their free perfection. These wilayah does not concern the infidel, the libertine, munafiqun and those who arc obstinate (towards Allah's commands) and they are outside the domain of this wilayah. In a sense, they have been left to themselves (by Allah)

At-Tawhid in the Value System of Islam

and only that very general divine planning governs them.

Al-Wilayatul-Khassah has very different stages. For example, the one who takes even a small step in the way of Allah and fulfills a small action for Allah, he will have a low stage of this guardianship and a limited share of divine favor will embrace him. Of course, if a mu'min makes proper use of this particular blessing of Allah and appreciates it, this very favor which has embraced him in the first stage, prepares him for taking a larger step and achieving greater growth and also causes him to receive more favor from Allah.

However, if he stops at this stage, he has enjoyed just this very stage of guardianship and will no longer reach higher stages. Anyhow, if a faithful person, i.e., a mu'min benefits from and makes good use of Divine Guardianship and takes more steps in the way of his own perfection, Allah will shower loftier favors upon him and in this way, these stages continue till they reach the most excellent position which a man may attain and that position is the sacred position of Allah's Wali and His Last Messenger, Prophet Muhammad ibn 'Abdullah (SA). Therefore, to the extent that man submits to Allah and makes his own will subject to Allah's will, and the more he uses Allah's blessings for his spiritual and real perfection, the more he will enjoy the blessing of divine guardianship.

The first step in the way of attaining divine guardianship is faith in Allah, pious deeds and struggle against taghut (Satan):

"...Therefore, whoever denies in the taghut and believes in Allah, he indeed has a strong hold on the firmest handle, which shall not break off; and Allah is Hearing, Knowing (2:256)."

Such a person has taken hold of the surest and firmest handle, and will save himself from perilous situations. In the continuation or the above ayah it said:

"Allah is the guardian of those who believe. He brings them out of the darkness into the light... (2:257)."

Those who believe in Allah and turn their back to taghut, Allah will undertake the planning of their affairs and takes them out of darkness and leads them towards light.

But those who are kafir are deprived of such guardianship, supervision and management and their supervision is with taghuts.

At-Tawhid in the Value System of Islam

> *"...And (to as) to those who disbelieve, their guardians are the taghuts... (2:257)."*

Faith and pious deeds which are conditions required for aptitude for divine guardianship and the enjoyment of Allah's particular favor, have different dimensions and stages and go ahead so far that Allah plans all the good for man, provides the means for their attainment and even more important than this, man reaches such a level where according to the following riwayat:

"The man reaches such a level where as if it is Allah who hears in place of his ear, and sees in place of his eyes and moves in place of his hands."[10]

It is obvious that Allah does not leave the affairs of such people to themselves, and rather He inspires them to what they should achieve through taking pains of experience and intellect, and even where their ordinary forces are not sufficient for the fulfillment of their affairs, Allah sends them divine hidden aids.

One dimension of divine guardianship is in relation to human societies and communities. Allah's planning and guardianship is sometimes for each and every one of human beings, and sometimes for

---

[10] "Al-'Usul al-Kafi", vol. 2, p. 352, Hadith 7 and Hadith 8 and the translated text of "Al-'Usul al-Kafi", vol. 4, p. 53 and 54.

the formation of divine communities which is fulfilled on a very extensive level and which has innumerable blessings. When Allah sees the merit for perfection in a people and observes some good in them, He provides the ground for their growth.

When human society achieved the aptitude for the emergence of the Holy Prophet (SA) of Islam, the Almighty Allah provided the grounds for the emergence of a monotheistic and Islamic society in the Arabian Peninsula. Allah created a man from the family of the past Prophets (AS), raised him so that at the age of forty he was appointed (by Allah) a Prophet and when a group of people came to believe in him and followed his way sincerely, Allah provided greater grounds for their growth and provided conditions so that they took steps towards perfection. Certain hardships occurred, sometimes people were troubled also, but Allah provides all grounds for the formation of a strong Islamic society, a society which can create a great development in the world.

Our Islamic Revolution was also like this. For centuries various conditions occurred for the Islamic society, Muslims had vacillations, peaks and abysses, until the Almighty Allah knew that a people in a country named Iran are ready for divine particular favor and from such people, a society can be made

At-Tawhid in the Value System of Islam

which can be the standard bearer of At-Tawhid throughout the earth.

Almighty Allah created a man from the family of the Prophets (AS) and the Infallible Imams (AS), raised him (to a lofty spiritual and intellectual level), taught him the required awareness, information and all- sided and comprehensive knowledge from Islam (of course through causes) and when a movement was to be started in the society, this man, (Al Imam AI-Khumayni (QS)) cried out his Tawhidi clamors and called on the people to move, till finally, in the year 1979 AD (1357 of the solar hijrah), they created a great resurrection (The Islamic Revolution of Iran) on the earth.

The particular divine guardianship is not limited to one stage and one phase and it can be said that it has innumerable stages, provided however that we properly observe the conditions for each stage and take more advantage of the possibilities which Allah The Almighty grants us and be thankful to Him for the blessing. (i.e., we use Allah's blessing in the way He Himself has ordained and we do not use them against His commands and will).

All that men should fulfill in the direction of benefiting from Allah's blessings and favors are summed up under one main title and that title is: "servitude to Allah".

> *"And that you should serve Me; this is the right way (36:61)".*

This servitude (to Allah) manifests itself in two general forms, one in the attainment of more understandings and the other in the performance of better actions.

At-Tawhid in Guidance

At-Tawhid in Rububiyyah has numerous branches. One of its branches is At-Tawhid in guidance. The leaching of the Holy Qur'an concerning the knowledge about At-Tawhid is that just: as the Almighty Allah has granted the existence to every being, He has also granted particular guidance to every being. After Musa (Moses) (AS) and Harun (Aaron) (AS) announced their call and Prophetic mission Fir'awn (Pharaoh) asked them: *"Who is that Lord to Whose worship you call me?"* Prophet Musa (AS) replied:

> *"...Our Lord is He Who gave to everything its creation, then guided it (20:50)".*

As the above ayah of the Holy Qur'an appears to indicate, just as creation has universality and includes every being, Divine guidance is also a general guidance which includes all beings. Of course we will later on elaborate that besides this general guidance which includes all beings, there is also a particular guidance which is particularly provided to mu'minun, just as it is the case with *wilayah*.

The general divine guidance has several parts; one the guidance which pertains to senseless creatures, such as material and natural creatures which have been created in this world. The other kind of guidance concerns sense-possessing creatures which have just one direction and are just active in that very direction, such as the angels (may greetings be upon them). The other kind of guidance is for the creatures which have animal sense and finally there is a guidance which concerns man - the being who besides the instinctive sense has the intellectual sense and in whose direction there are two different ways of which he selects one.

To give more explanation for these parts, it should be said that each being which is created in this world, from the smallest particle to the greatest galaxies, so far as man's knowledge and information have reached them, has a particular effect and movement which have been placed in a determined direction.

The smallest particle which man has known so far is called an atom. Inside an atom there is a nucleus around which small particles named electrons revolve. This movement is a particular movement in a determined axis and particular direction. Allah The Omnipotent has created this invisible, little and tiny particle such that the electrons traverse their own way inside it and never follow any way against the direction Allah has determined for them and the electrons do not go out of their axis/orbit unduly.

This orderliness is on the basis of the law which Allah has placed in the nature of this being and for this reason we call it a creational and natural guidance, namely, these effects and movements, with particular directions and special qualities are all subject to the creation the Almighty Allah has granted them.

After the atoms, there are the molecules which are formed of a number of atoms, the formation of molecules which takes place with particular composition, condition and manner, so that particular effects of them would be realized in the world is also a kind of divine creational guidance. Molecules gradually turn into a complicated form and are combined and from them various matters come into being.

In chemistry, there is a wonderful story of how the atoms are put together in a particular way and how these atoms bring into existence these various objects with great and complicated properties. Really, Who has created these things in such a way and has put these properties in them that they rest beside each other in such ways?

After mineral and chemical matters, we enter the world of plants. The stone of a tree is put in the earth. It uses the moisture and heat of the earth. Gradually, the shell of this stone split, a root is sent inside the earth and a stem is sent out of the ground and the next stages which a plant goes through from the start to the end follow.

This is the law and guidance Allah The Almighty has put in the world of plants according to which they absorb the food particles from the earth, combine and analyze them, so that they partly turn into leaves and partly into branches. The more we study about the world of plants, the more wonderfully we will observe the signs of Divine guidance.

In the world of animals, divine guidance emerges in more strange form. Among plants, we did not know of any sense, though it has been said that some plants have a weak sense. For example, among trees it is known that the palm trees have a weak sense, or that some plants are carnivorous and hunt their prey with their leaves, in the way that when an animal sits on their leaves, the leaves contract, draw that animal inside themselves, digest it and grow in this way, but generally in plants we do not recognize and know of such senses (intelligence) and even if it does exist, we cannot distinguish,

But, there are other groups of beings in whom the signs of senses (intelligence) are quite clearly apparent and everybody can understand that such beings possess particular senses. A chicken, as soon as it comes out of the egg, goes under the wings of its mother; if it feels cold, and hits with its peck at the ground, if it feels hungry. Each kind of animals has its particular senses.

There are some fish that go hundreds of kilometers in the sea to reach a place which is fit for laying eggs and where their eggs are not destroyed, and then they return. The fish which come out of the eggs and open their eyes to the sea for the first time traverse the same route their mothers have traversed and return to their place. One of the animals about which the Holy Qur'an has particularly discussed is the bee.

The particular sense of this animal in making hexagonal houses and its providing its food from various flowers and blossoms, its storing them and the other phases of its life are distinguished proofs for this claim. Also there are birds which make nests for themselves for the first time, without having seen it (being made) anywhere before.

For instance, we see that swallows make nests in a particular from in the roofs of houses, in a safe place and lay eggs there, and/or we see that domestic hens, after laying eggs, sleep on them and every now and then turn them over. If the hen were asked why it sleeps on the eggs, perhaps it had no reply to give, of course we do not know of the inside of the soul of the hen and do not know what senses and understandings it has. But it seems very probable that it does not have a logical answer for this action, only a desire is created inside it that drives it to such acts.

These are divine teachings and guidance. No one has taught such things to hens and to thousands of kinds of animals each of which has particular characteristics, rather Allah has revealed to them. About such kinds of instinctive guidance's, the Holy Qur'an applies the expression Wahy (divine revelation).

> "And Your Lord revealed to the bee... (16:68)".

At-Tawhid: Monotheism

This is a mysterious and unknown learning which is not understandable for the others and which is developed in the inside of the animal.

The other kind of guidance is for the sense-possessing beings which have but one direction, such as the angels (greetings be upon them). They are very noble and intelligent beings, but they fulfill their actions only at Allah's command.

> *"...Nay! They are honoured servants: they do not precede Him in speech and (only) according to His commandment do they act (21:26,27)".*

This group of creatures whose being we understand just through the information given by the Almighty Allah and the Infallibles (AS), have particular guidance and perform the very action which Allah -The Almighty has determined for them and of which the way of performance He has taught them.

There is a group of the angels whose function is to write down the actions of men. Allah has created them for this very action and has also taught them how to fulfill their function and from the beginning of creation up to now, their work has been and will be this. The other groups (of the angels) are in charge of means of subsistence and the third group in charge of the other works of creation.

The kind of angels mentioned in the Holy Qur'an have each a specific position, special work and particular guidance and they are all engaged in praising, glorifying and extolling Allah.

> "...And we celebrate Thy praise and extol Thy holiness... (2:30)."

Though in the Holy Qur'an the sort of praising (Allah) and even acts of worship and prayers have been proved for all beings, but we do not really understand how birds in the sky perform prayers or praise Allah.

The Holy Qur'an says:

> "...He knows the prayer of each one and its glorification... (24:41)."

In another place, the Holy Qur'an says:

> "...And there is not a single thing but glorifies Him with His praise, but you do not understand their glorification... (17:44)."

The Guidance Particular to Man

Amidst these guidance's man is blessed with an excellent guidance. Man is an essence of the whole system of creation; right from the characteristics of atoms, molecules, protein and chemical matters to the vegetal, animal and instinctive characteristics are all found in his being. But above all these things, there is a guidance which has privileged and distinguished him from other creatures and which has made him superior even to angels, and that is the power of the intellect which the Almighty Allah has bestowed in man's being so that he can understand certain facts both in theoretical dimension and the practical one.

In regard to man, mere instinctive inspiration, which exists in animals, has not been contented with. Of course human infant has an instinctive understanding too. For example, it knows how to suck its mother's breast and when feeling pain, how to make known its pain through crying and groaning. This is an instinctive sense which exists in animals too. But on man's reaching maturity, another sense appears in him, the like of which does not exist too to such an extent in animals. Man, being possessed with this characteristic, makes intellectual analyses and logical reasoning's, becomes informed about unseen facts and finds out about their existence.

We know that scientists have assumed in their minds many of the scientific theories without having any information about their external existence and then proved the same with analogies and experience, Man

At-Tawhid in the Value System of Islam

even possesses such an ability that through intellect besides innate understanding and the knowledge which is acquired not through using the five senses but through illumination into the heart, can achieve a conscious and acquired understanding towards the Almighty Allah and His attributes and best names and this is a very great and noble power and very constructive and significant for man's perfection.

Also, in the practical part, human intellect has the ability to distinguish good and bad, praiseworthy and indecent in doings and actions. Allah has put this power in man to recognize both the good directions and the bad ones, to know both the way of impiety and the way of virtuousness, to recognize both the way or justice and truth and the way of oppression, tyranny and injustice: and with profound insight he can select any one he wishes.

The Holy Qur'an says:

> "Surely We have shown him the way: he may be thankful or unthankful (76:3)."

Thus without any thing being compulsorily imposed upon him to acquire perfection of his truth with his own choice.

The existence of the power of intellect causes man to recognize the generalities of the matters and the main lines of truth and falsehood, but in detailed and minute cases, he needs another form of guidance.[11] Allah - The Wise Who has created man for voluntary perfection, has not spared him such guidance either and has compensated for the defect in his understanding and recognition by Wahy and Nubuwwah.

Thus, to the first man (Adam (AS)) He created, besides giving him the power of intellect, Allah also made revelation and ordained him one of the Prophets, and later Almighty Allah also appointed other Prophets (AS) according to what His wisdom demanded, so that the deficiencies in the insights of the intellect in theoretical and practical grounds, which are needed by men, are compensated.

So, in reality, the greatest blessing the Almighty Allah has granted man is this particular guidance which is summed up in two parts, one the guidance of the intellect and the other the guidance of the Wahy. In other words, Almighty Allah has ordained

---

[11] Intellect does not have the ability to perceive all the details of the matters. For example, all wise men know that justice is good and oppression is bad. But they cannot distinguish the details of the cases of justice and oppression, that exactly where is oppression and where is justice? The matter might reach to such a point where the truth and falsehood -justice and oppression- are mistaken for each other and the truth is regarded as falsehood and justice as oppression.

two kinds of proof and guide for men: one the inner proof, namely, the intellect and since this proof was not sufficient, Allah has also arranged another proof outside the being of the individuals, (namely, the Prophets (AS)) which compensates for the deficiency in the insight of the intellect.

So far, for the general guidance's, i.e., the guidance's of the contents of which both the mu'min and the kafir, the virtuous and the un-virtuous can be informed, but just as the guardianship of Allah over the creatures has two parts; one the general guardianship which includes the mu'min and the kafir equally, and the other guardianship which is particular to the mu'min and of which guardianship the kafirun have no share, the same is also true of guidance. That is, besides the general guidance, there is another form of guidance particular to the mu'min the honor of which only includes those who sincerely tread the way of servitude to Allah.

After the reaching of the guidance of the wahy to the people, people divide towards it into two groups: One group being those people who accept the divine guidance and believe in the wahy and in the prophet-hood and who also follow the orders of the Prophets (AS) in performing their deeds.

The other group of people, with their wrong choice, ignores and disregards this guidance and do not put it as the source of effect in their lives. These two groups, though each will receive the reward (or the torment) for their good and bad actions, it will not be the same in this very world either. Upon those who are thankful for the blessing of guidance, who behaves in the way Allah has commanded and who know the value of this blessing, Allah increases His blessing:

> "And (as for) those who follow the right direction, He increases them in guidance... (47:17)."

And in contrast, as for those who are unthankful, Allah will turn their hearts away from the truth.

> "...But when they turned aside, Allah made their hearts turn aside... (61:5)."

But the Holy Qur'an depicts the way of achieving this true guidance:

> "...There has come to you light and a clear Book from Allah; with it Allah guides him who will follow His pleasure into the ways of safety... (5:15-16)."

Those attain true guidance who possess this spiritual and cordial condition, namely, being desirous and in

At-Tawhid in the Value System of Islam

search of Allah's pleasure and satisfaction and this condition is not achieved unless with possessing the following levels: Faith, holding fast to Allah in action and love for Allah and it is in the wake of these attainments that man attempts to acquire Allah's pleasure and satisfaction and such men will enjoy the spiritual light of the Holy Qur'an and the particular divine guidance. This guidance is just and only just in Allah's hand and It is He Who creates such a light in their hearts,

Therefore, to be able to benefit both from the particular divine guidance and also to be embraced by particular Allah's guardianship, we should appreciate Allah's blessings, abandon egotism and replace it with theism and Godliness. This will not be achieved by mere slogans, nor is it acquired by just performing the prayers. Rather, one's heart should be submitted to Allah and also the motives out of which one acts should be Divine and self-centrism and groupism should be wiped out of one's life and one's goal and objective should become just his perfection as well as the others' perfection. One should desire Allah's guidance for himself and for the others and in this way desire nothing but Allah's pleasure and in one word, one should submit his being totally to Allah:

> *"And whoever submits himself wholly to Allah and he is the doer of good (to others), he indeed has taken hold of the firmest thing upon which one can lay hold... (31:22)."*

Such a man acquires the merit for acquiring the blessing of Allah's particular guidance; otherwise due to being unthankful for the blessing, the blessing will be taken away (from him) by Allah.

Providing Sustenance

Another branch or dimension of At-Tawhid in Rububiyyah which has been greatly emphasized in the Holy Qur'an is that Almighty Allah is the Only One Who provides sustenance to His creatures and provides for their needs. The Holy Qur'an says:

> *"O' men! Call to mind the favor of Allah on you; is there any creator besides Allah who gives you sustenance from the heaven and the earth? There is no god but He; whence are you then turned away?"*
> *(35:3)*

As is observed, in the above ayah of the Holy Qur'an, being the Creator and being the Giver of sustenance have been regarded as being necessarily accompanying each other. The Holy Qur'an says: *"Is there any creator besides Allah who gives you sustenance?"* This contains a very delicate point. As a

At-Tawhid in the Value System of Islam

rule, it might seem that the question should have been put in the following way: *"Is there a giver of sustenance who gives you sustenance?"*

However, the Holy Qur'an puts the question in this way: "Is there any creator besides Allah who gives you sustenance'?' This ayah of the Holy Qur'an points out the fact that giving sustenance is one of the prestigious matters of creation; namely, means of sustenance (including food) should have been created in the world so that when a creature needs any means of sustenance, for example food, he can have access to it, use it and continue his life.

So, in reality, it can be said that The One Who has created him in need of means of sustenance and Who has put the means of sustenance, including foodstuffs within his reach, is the same One Who gives sustenance to him and in fact giving sustenance is nothing but the fact that he can use the foodstuffs which have been created and which have been put within his reach.

Of course the word "rizq" (sustenance) is sometimes applied in a more extensive sense which also includes non - material sustenance's. For instance, it is said that the sustenance for the soul is knowledge or even about the angels there is a riwayat that: *"and their food is praising (Allah)"*. But by sustenance which is discussed here, material sustenance for the continuation of worldly and a perfect life is meant which depends on sustenance. One of men's reproachable characteristics is that as long as they feel in need and sense their hunger, thirst, and their other material needs, they stretch out their hands towards Allah, but when their needs are met, they become neglectful of Allah, particularly if they have themselves made an effort or applied their mental and scientific capabilities (in connection with meeting the needs). In this connection, the Holy Qur'an says:

"So when harm afflicts a man he calls upon Us, then, when we give him a favor from Us, he says: 'I have been given it only by means of knowledge'. Nay, it is a trial, but most of them do not know (39:49)."

The Almighty Allah showered His blessings on some of His creatures, but they imagined that these blessings have been achieved as a result of their own endeavors, cleverness, sagacity, knowledge and intelligence.

One of the distinguished examples of such persons is Qarun (Koran, Croesus). About the wealth of Qarun there are many stories. The Holy Qur'an talks about his wealth in the following verse:

> *"...And We had given him of the treasures, so much so that his hoards of wealth would certainly weigh down a company of men possessed of great strength... (28:76)."*

The pious people admonished Qarun and said to him:

> *"And seek by means of what Allah has given you the future abode, and do not neglect your portion of this world... (28:77)."*

The pious people advised him not to become proud of these riches, not to make them means of mischief on the earth and to try to use the bounties Allah had given him for his life in the Hereafter. But in reply to them, Qarun said:

> *"I have been given this only on account of the knowledge I have... (28:78)."*

So, Qarun's response was: *"Which wealth has Allah given me'? I myself have endeavored and acquired the wealth with my knowledge and industry and no one has any right in my wealth. The poor and the subdued should themselves go and get money."*

Such attitude, namely, to think that what we achieve is due to our own endeavors and efforts, and that

At-Tawhid: Monotheism

our achievements are of our own is the very polytheistic attitude und a muwahhid should know that his being is from Allah, his physical power, his intellectual power and all the matters in which he brings about changes are all from Allah, and still more, using the same is also depending upon Allah's planning and it is not the case that anybody who has gathered wealth and acquired some riches, will be able to use that wealth well in this world.

There might he many who amassed lots of wealth (whether in a halal (lawful by Islam) or in a haram (unlawful by Islam) way), but did not succeed in using this wealth. Qarun was also rated among such persons. He could not use the immense wealth he had amassed, because Allah's torment fell upon him and both he and his wealth were swallowed up by the earth (at Allah's command). Those who desired to have Qarun's wealth, when saw this event, became conscious of the fact that merely possessing wealth and worldly riches is not sufficient for felicity in this world.

"And those who yearned for his place only the day before began to say, 'Ah! (know) that Allah increases and straitens the means of subsistence for whom He wills of His servants'... (28:82)."

They saw that all that wealth sank in the earth and nothing of it was won by Qarun and that even he himself perished. They said that: *'Ah! it seems that it is Allah Who increases the means of subsistence for anybody He wills and straitens it for anybody He wills'*, This matter, (namely, the increasing and straitening of (he means of subsistence) has been clearly stipulated in over ten ayat of the Holy Qur'an, including the following Ayah:

> "Allah increases and straitens the means of subsistence for whom He wills... (13:26)."

The planning of the means of subsistence, increasing it or straitening it is all in Allah's hand.

Allah's Predestination in Men's Sustenance

Of course it is not the case that Allah decreases or increases anybody's means of sustenance without expedience and wisdom, and if some persons' means of subsistence are increased or decreased, it is on the basis of Allah's wise rules and principles. The Holy Qur'an says:

> "And if Allah should amplify the provision for His servants they would certainly revolt in the earth; but He sends it down according to a measure as He pleases; surely He is Aware of, Seeing, His servants (42:27)."

The Holy Qur'an says that if Allah amplified men's means of subsistence to such an extent that there would be no need for them to endeavor and try, these men would become rebellious, so Allah sends down the means of subsistence to the extent He knows advisable and It is He Who is Aware of the situation of His creatures and knows all that is expedient for each.

Besides the more important point is that the existence of various means of subsistence and their being less and more is one of the Divine tests as the Holy Qur'an says:

"...And raised some of you above others by (various) grades, that He might try you by what He has given you... (6:165)."

And above this, basically all the affairs of the life in this world are the means for a test.

"Who created death and life that He may try you- which of you is the best in deeds... (67:2)."

As for the manner of testing, we know that people are not equal in physical force and not all can perform one kind of economic activity at the same level: One has more physical power and the other less.

Likewise, people's mental power and their management abilities are not the same, In the midst of all this, those who have less physical and mental power, enjoy less material shares and naturally those who have more mental, scientific and administrative powers, gain more products and willy-nilly people' means of subsistence become different.

The Almighty Allah, with this difference in means of subsistence. tests the men that whether individuals arc contented with their own rights or extend the hands of aggression to the rights of the others; whether the one who has lots of wealth, supposing that he has also acquired that wealth through halal ways, fulfills his duties or whether like Qarun, he says:

> *"I have been given this only on account of the knowledge I have... (28:78)."*

And, in the other case. whether he worships Allah only when he has wealth or whether even if his wealth is taken away from him, he still remembers Allah; and whether a person beseeches Allah and extends his hands of prayer, benediction and appealing to Allah just when he is empty-handed and has no wealth or whether he remembers Allah when he is rich too? Therefore, the difference between means of subsistence and people's enjoying different blessings is a general wisdom by which people are tested and tried.

Reasons For and Causes of Change of Subsistence

But sometimes the cause of change of means of subsistence is the individual himself, in the way that if an individual appreciates a God-given blessing, makes good use of it and treads the path of Allah, that blessing will be increased for him:

> "...If you are grateful, I would certainly give to you more... (14:7)."

And likewise, being ungrateful for the blessings and not treating the God-given blessings in a thankful way, will cause the straitening and decrease in the blessings and will be followed by Allah's torment and displeasure:

> "...And if you are ungrateful, My chastisement is truly severe... (14:7)."

Of course, this misconception should not occur either that if anybody has more blessings, it indicates that he is fulfilling Allah's commands better, for, there are many who not only do not appreciate Allah's blessings, but who also misuse the same and attempt to obstinately oppose and fight

At-Tawhid in the Value System of Islam

against the truth and the true servants of Allah, as are the superpowers of the world today, and yet Allah does not take His blessings away from them, but sometimes even increases those blessings upon them.

This is another divine Sunnah (tradition) called imla' (giving respite) and istidraj (drawing one towards a failure situation), that is, if some people, due to their own wrong choice, follow the path of falsehood and continue to tread on it rapidly and severely and there is no hope of their returning (to Allah's way), Allah will, through increasing the material blessings, provide the grounds for their spiritual collapse, their peace and tranquility are taken away from them and eventually eternal torment will be brought about for them. In this regard, the Holy Qur'an says:

> *"And let not those who disbelieve think that Our granting them respite is better for them; We grant them respite so that they increase their sins... (3:178)."*

The Holy Qur'an warns us against imagining that when Allah gives some blessings to the disbelievers, these blessings will do well for them. According to the Holy Qur'an, this is not at all the case and rather Allah increases the blessings for them so that they will be polluted with more sins and be afflicted with more torment both in this world and in the hereafter.

One of the other divine traditions in planning for men is the tradition of helping. That is, if someone, of his own free will, chooses to follow the way of mischief, Allah, too, will help him to proceed further in that way and if he chooses the way of goodness, Allah, too, will help him to become better. The Holy Qur'an says:

"All do We aid— these as well as those— out of the bounty of your Lord, and the bounty of your Lord is not confined (17:20)."

According to the Holy Qur'an, both the ones who turn into worshipers of this world's life and who turn their whole attention to the material pleasures and also those who devote themselves to the love for Allah and the truth and who tread the path of human perfections, are aided and helped by Allah. The help to the world -worshipers is that they are let more deeply drown in the world and become more neglectful of Allah and the help to the believers and the seekers of the truth is that their insight and spirituality are increased, their faith is exalted and through the fulfillment of more pious deeds, their spiritual degrees and other worldly perfections are increased.

So, Allah's giving means of subsistence to His creatures and His increasing and decreasing the same arc under particular laws, regulations and principles of which some were pointed out here. However, we are not aware of the formula of many others (of these laws, regulations and principles). Briefly it can be said that Allah gives, whatever He knows expedient and His wisdom demands, to anybody anywhere. For some people expedience demands amplification of the means of subsistence and for some, straitening of the means of subsistence is demanded by expedience.

Likewise, in the Holy Qur'an certain causes and traditions have also been expressed for straitening the means of subsistence. One of those traditions is being ungrateful for the blessings. The Holy Qur'an says:

"And Allah sets forth a parable: (Consider) a town safe and secure to which its means of subsistence come in abundance from every quarter; but it became ungrateful to Allah's favors, therefore Allah made it to taste the utmost degree of hunger and fear because of what they wrought (16:112)."

In the above verse of the Holy Qur'an, Allah sets forth as a parable, a people who lived in a fertile land and for whom there were plenty of blessings and besides, to whom blessings came from other places too and who lived in the utmost degree of happiness, ease and plenty, until they became ungrateful for Allah's blessings, used them in improper ways, spoiled and wasted them and in one word, did not fulfill their duties in regard to Allah's blessing. For this reason, the garb of hunger and insecurity were put on them and they tasted poverty and misery and this was the punishment for the bad deeds they had committed.

Sometimes, too, the means of subsistence are straitened (by Allah) for testing (the people). There is a man who is a believer, who obeys Allah's commands, and who is not ungrateful for Allah's blessings either, but who should be tested for his perfection, (i.e., so that he will achieve perfection). Prophet Ayyub (may Allah's blessings be upon him) is one of the great and praiseworthy Prophets of Allah who has a very lofty position.

The Almighty Allah, for increasing his degrees, made him the object of a severe test and trial and took away from him the material blessings. But this worthy servant of Allah, in all the hardships was greatly patient and rendered forbearance and did not speak even a word of complaint and he reached (such a lofty) position that the Almighty Allah, concerning his status has made a statement which He has made about few Prophets:

"...Surely We found him patient; most excellent the servant! ... (38:44)."

One of the other reasons for the straitening of the means of subsistence is the people's negligence of their duty towards the deprived and the poor. In this connection, the Holy Qur'an says:

"And as for man, when his Lord tries him, then treats him with honor and makes him lead an easy life, he says: My Lord honors me. But when He tries him (differently), then straitens to him his means of subsistence, he says: My Lord has disgraced me (89:15-16)."

Here (in the above ayat), it is well observed that in both cases first the "trial" has been emphasized; the "trial" sometimes has the form of an amplification of the means or subsistence and sometimes the form of straitening it. The Holy Qur'an says that if Allah grants man the blessing of honor, makes him respected and honorable in the society and gives him lots of blessings, he says: *"1 am very dear In Allah for He has given so many blessings to me."*

But if his means of subsistence is straitened, it is here that he says: *"Allah has disgraced me"*. But this is not true, because both are "trials", both, that is, amplification of the means of subsistence and the straitening of the means of subsistence. But this straitening of the means of subsistence and becoming disgraced, is the punishment for the actions man has himself performed.

"Nay! But you do not honor the orphan; Nor do you urge one another to feed the poor; and you eat away the heritage, devouring (everything) indiscriminately; and you love wealth with exceeding love (89:17-20)."

The Holy Qur'an says that you did not honor the people's orphans and discriminated between them and your own children that you did not urge one another to feed and tend to the poor. (The Holy Qur'an does not say *"and you do not feed the poor"*, the significance of feeding the poor, is preserved in its own place and anybody who has the ability should tend to the poor and the needy, rather above this, according to the Holy Qur'an, you should urge one another to tend to the poor and the needy, so that through cooperation, co-thinking and urging each other, a remedy will be worked out for social poverty).

The Holy Qur'an says that with your strange attachment and love for wealth, you indiscriminately devoured the wealth inherited from your fathers and relatives and even did not give part of it to the poor, to your neighbors and to your relatives. These caused the leaf of your trial to change and your means of subsistence to be straitened.

Providing Sustenance Through Uncommon Ways

The point which needs to be pointed out here is that besides granting the means of subsistence in an ordinary way and through the causes and the means, Allah is able to provide sustenance without the natural means and in an exceptional way, as was the case tor Maryam (AS). The Holy Qur'an says:

> "...And Zakariyya took charge of her; whenever Zakariyya called upon her at the sanctuary, he found food with her. He said, "O Maryam! whence comes this to you?" She said: "It is from Allah. Surely Allah gives to whom He wills without measure" (3:37)."

Among the pious men and 'ulama' of this ummah, too, such miracles and stories exist in plenty which if collected, will form a voluminous encyclopedia. However, Allah's wisdom demands that man be always exposed to test and that his perfection is fulfilled by the way of his own choice and selection.

If people saw their food ready and descended from heavens each day, they would feel no need and would not realize the fact that they are creatures who are totally in need. If people did not have to endeavor for achieving their means of subsistence, these sciences and industries would not develop in the world and divine wisdoms and the mysteries of Allah in creation would not be known in their light and naturally neither material progress, nor spiritual evolution would be attained by man.

If everybody's means of subsistence reached him without his taking pains and going through difficulties and if it were not necessary for him to work and engage in activities, the matter of halal and haram would not be propounded in business and trade and it would not become known whether a person makes aggression upon other people's property or not? Whether in business dealings he speaks the truth or he cheats! Whether when enjoying Allah's blessings, he pays the others' rights or not and whether he helps the poor, the relatives, the kin's and the needy and many other such possibilities which become known just through testing and trial in different forms and manners.

Therefore, behind endeavoring and being tested, there are certain wisdoms which if they did not exist, the way of so many perfections would remain closed to man.

Divine Wisdom

At the conclusion of this section, namely, the section on the clarification of At-Tawhid in the ideological system (of Islam), we pay to the discourse that all divine planning's are wise, of course, great Divine scholars have discussed this matter in detail and written many books, but here we will just content ourselves with a simple expression.

When we know Allah and come to believe that firstly; Allah is aware of future events: secondly; Allah is able to create any creature the way He wants to; thirdly: Allah loves good and perfection and since good and perfection are rays or the perfection of His Being and are desired and loved by Him, He creates His creatures with great goodness and perfection; fourthly: Allah docs not envy His creatures and in other words, when we believe in Allah's knowledge, power, good-will and His being not envious, we conclude that the world has been created in the best condition of goodness, perfection and expedience and it is planned in the most possible suitable manner.

The Holy Qur'an, too, explicitly points out this matter and says:

> "Who made good everything that He has created... (32:7)."

At another place the Holy Qur'an says:

> "...The handiwork of Allah Who has made everything thoroughly; surely He is Aware of what you do (27:88)."

Allah's handiwork is such that He has created everything in a firm and concrete form and in the best manner and without vacuum. He has placed in creatures everything that wisdom demands and has not rendered any stinginess and parsimony.

In the face of this general principle, namely, the divine wisdom and the fact that the planning of the world and of man is in the best way, naturally, some questions may occur to individuals as to which wisdom is involved in each particular case?, though It is an undue expectation and man does not have the ability to understand and realize all secrets and wisdoms:

> "...And you are not given aught of knowledge but a little (17:85)."

However, Allah has generally expressed certain principles in the Holy Qur'an and on the basis of those general principles we can, with the guidance of wahy interpret many of the phenomena and discover, to the extent of our ability, the wisdoms behind them. But a faithful person, should both on the basis of logical reason and also on the basis of the verses of the Holy Qur'an, possesses this confidence that whatever happens, in any place it happens and in any form it happens, it is the demand of the wisdom of creation and that were it other than this, it would be against (divine) wisdom.

The Wisdom Behind Bearing Difficulties by Man

One of the most important principles behind men's bearing difficulties and hardships is the blossoming of the talents and the actualization of their hidden potentialities, so that whereby they attain their worthy perfection. For instance, just as physical growth and physical power come into being in the light of severe exercises (by the individual), and the one who wishes to have more physical power should do more and harder exercises, so also the growth of spiritual perfections is acquired through entering the field of difficulties and hardships and bearing them, and by this means man's God-given talents turn into reality.

In the language of the Holy Qur'an, providing the grounds for spiritual practices is called "testing", "ibtila", "imtahan", "fitna" and similar expressions which have been pointed out in the Holy Qur'an are viewing these very events which occur for men due to divine planning and predestination.

In fact, what is called "test" in the language of the Holy Qur'an is also raising and in this respect, we can call the world a place of raising besides a place of testing, because man's talents are raised in the world and in the world his potential abilities arc actualized. In the riwayat, it has been said that the Almighty Allah tests the mu'min (the faithful person) by means of hardships and difficulties, as a mother raises her child by suckling it.

However, the Holy Qur'an, among the above meanings, has pointed out another fact in connection with these divine tests and that fact is that if a person passes his test well and is properly raised in this place of raising and gets good marks, besides achieving certain levels of spiritual perfection and growth, he becomes a model for the others too and attains the position of men's leadership and imamah. So, one of the goals behind

At-Tawhid in the Value System of Islam

tests which is the very existence of hardships and difficulties is that among men, individuals emerge who will be examples for the others (to follow).

Such divine goals behind putting forth hardships and testing men, are depict able in three forms: one, a distinguished person grows in the society and attains high positions and the others follow him. This, being model and parable, has many levels, its higher level being the level of the exalted prophets (AS) and the Infallible Imams (AS), the very level which Allah - The Almighty has granted to Prophet Ibrahim (Abraham) (AS). In the following ayah which we have repeatedly heard,

"And when Ibrahim's Lord tried with (certain) words, he fulfilled them. He said: Surely I will make you an Imam (religious leader)... (2:124)."

After (granting) the position of Nubuwwah, risalah (being a Messenger of Allah) and Khullat (being a friend of Allah) (all of which were wonderful positions the Almighty Allah had granted to Hazrat Ibrahim (AS)), when willing to grant a higher position to Ibrahim (AS) the Almighty Allah tested him. Thus, Ibrahim (AS) was first afflicted with the fire of the men of Numrud (Nimrod). This was one stage of the test after successfully passing which he

At-Tawhid: Monotheism

achieved the needed readiness for accepting the position of Imamah.

In the riwayat it has been said that when Ibrahim (AS) was been put in the fire, Jibra'il (the archangel Gabriel) came to him and said:

"Do you want any help?"

Ibrahim (AS) said: *"I do need help. I am totally in need, Every creature, every being is nothing but in want and in need. But not from you?"*[12] This was the first test for Ibrahim (AS) that whether he, under such hard conditions would extend his hands for want to even Jibra'il (AS) or not?

In another stage of the test, Ibrahim (AS) was asked (by Allah) to take his wife (Hajar (AS)) and his beloved child (Isma'il) (AS)) in a dry wilderness, in the Hijaz deserts of Makkah. As per Allah's command, Ibrahim (AS) made his family migrate to this land, left them there, and tolerated the pains of separation for the sake of the pleasure of the Almighty Allah.

The third test, which was at the same time, the hardest of them too, was the test to which Ibrahim (AS) was put at old age (at the time when his

---

[12] "Biharul-Anwar", vol. 2, p. 39, Hadith 24.

physical capability was reduced, the Almighty Allah granted a son, named, Isma'il to him and naturally he enjoyed seeing such a son and having companionship and association with him.). Ibrahim (AS) was commanded (by Allah) to cut off with his own hands the head of his young son (Isma'il (AS)) who was then at the peak of fruitfulness, handsomeness, perfection and worthiness. This is a very hard and a very great test. But without any hesitation, Ibrahim (AS) told his son that he had such a command. Isma'il (AS), too, responded:

"...O my father! Do what you are commanded; if Allah please, you will find me of the patient ones (37:102)."

It is here that such a person who has tolerated hardships and offered all he had in the way of Allah should become an Imam and model for the others.

Likewise, some of the other great Prophets (AS), after bearing certain hardships attained the position of Imamah who have been briefly referred to in the following ayah of the Holy Qur'an:

"And We made of them Imams to guide by Our command when they were patient... (32:24)."

At-Tawhid: Monotheism

Also sometimes a group of the society becomes a model for other groups. If in a society, the people adorned with goodness, moral soundness and piety voluntarily embrace hardships and difficulties, dispense with comfort, ease and welfare of life and direct their efforts towards serving Allah's creatures; such a group of the society acquires the position of leadership and becomes an example and model for the others.

However, above all this is that when an Ummah (Islamic people) becomes a model for the other people; if the people collectively achieve its goodness and successfully passes its test, the whole of this people becomes a pattern for the other people and just as it has been ordained by Divine will that among each Ummah (people), a distinguished individual, the distinguished individuals, or a distinguished group undertakes the leadership of the others, so also it has been ordained by the Divine Will that among all human societies, a society be realized which will be a model for all human societies.

This (Divine) Will, at the present age, has ordained that our Islamic Ummah, should rise up in this land (in the Islamic Republic of Iran), pass the tests one after the other, pass the tests of Khurdad 15, 1342 SH (solar Hijrah) (June 5, 1963 AD), the test of Bahman

22, 1357 SH (February 11, 1979 AD), of the war, of the economic siege, the back-breaking tragically events, problems and hardships successfully and honorably and with hands overflowing with matchless self-sacrifice, epic and resistance,[13] attain the position of leadership, and become a pattern and model for other nations and its people.

The other wisdom behind the existence of hardships and troubles is that man comes to notice the fact that the worldly life is not an ideal life and that man's innate ideal which is eternal perfection and felicity is not possible in this world. Man's eyes, due to his weakness of recognition, particularly in the primary stages of life and before being trained by Allah's Prophets (AS) and Allah's awliya' (AS) are fixed at material pleasures and worldly enjoyments, and that which he primarily understands and recognizes are these very pleasures of this world's life and he knows no other thing; whereas, if this world's life was totally for pleasures and comforts, it would cause man to go astray.

---

[13] In one of the towns of our Islamic country which is a relatively small town too, two hundred missiles were hit, rendering the town into the form of a ruin. However, the people of this town say: "We wish the missiles and bombs too which hit the other towns and cities of our country would hit our town, so that the people of the other towns and cities would remain safe and sound." Where in history has self-sacrifice been witnessed?

So, on the basis of Allah's wisdom, there should be hardships in this world to warn man that what he truly demands and what his inborn nature desires, namely, 'eternal felicity', is not possible in this world. Therefore, the existence of disasters and problems in this world's life is for man to take lesson, for him not to become infatuated with this world, not to be entrapped by its pleasures and luxuries and to know that this life is a means for testing, that here is a bridge for passing and a passage which should be passed by and left, for the eternal felicity.

Another fact of wisdom pointed out in the Holy Qur'an is the fact that when man is engaged in enjoyment and comfort and all that he wants is provided for him, he does not notice his weakness and needfulness and consequently the seeds of rebellion and disobedience (towards Allah's Commands) grow in his soul, leading him towards selfishness and egoism and he gradually forgets Allah.

> "Nay! Man is most surely inordinate; Because he sees himself free from want (96:6-7)."

Therefore, Allah must, on the basis of His supreme wisdom, make men realize their needfulness in various conditions and with various methods and

At-Tawhid in the Value System of Islam

make them notice the fact that they are thoroughly in need so that by this means their hearts turn to Allah. This general rule has been expressed by the Allah in two verses of the Holy Qur'an, saying that He has sent no Prophets to any people, but first having afflicted that people with hardships and troubles, so that the grounds for paying attention towards Allah and the state of modesty, humbleness and entreaty (towards Allah) occurs for them.

"And certainly We sent (Messengers) to nations before you, then We seized them with distress and affliction in order that they might humble themselves (6:42)."

In another verse, Allah, with a more explicit and decisive tone, says:

"And We did not send a Prophet in a town but We overtook its people with distress and affliction in order that they might humble themselves (7:94)."

In the former Ayah (6:42), it is said (by Allah) that *(and certainly We sent)*, but in the latter Ayah (7:94), Allah in a language which points to a particular case says that:

"And We did not send a prophet in a town but We overtook its people with distress and afflictions... "

So, another Divine wisdom behind the existence of disasters and problems in life is that man gets into the state of humbling himself (before Allah) and beseeching (to Him) and feeling of being in need and does not become proud of the blessings Allah has put at his disposal.

He does not think that they belong to himself, that he himself has acquired them and that whenever he wishes, the blessings will be provided for him with his own efforts, and that man knows that this is not the case, that Allah's planning is above these planning's and that sometimes in spite of all his efforts and endeavors, he still becomes afflicted with hardship.

One of the other of these wisdoms is the understanding (by man) of the significance of the blessings, for, if all blessings are provided for man and his needs are met, he becomes neglectful and fails to understand their significance. A simple example serves well to clarify this matter: All of us use the air and know that the greatest needs of life for each living being are air and water. If the oxygen of the air does not reach us, our life will be endangered in a few seconds. But how many times, have each of us in our life-time said to Allah: "*O Allah, thanks to You for having created the air.*" Few are those who notice the fact that the air too is a

At-Tawhid in the Value System of Islam

great blessing, because it is and has always been at our disposal.

So that people would know the value of His blessings and endeavor to be thankful, whereby attaining perfection and providing the ground for their being endowed with the ever-lasting eternal blessings, Allah sometimes brings about certain vacillations in the existence of the blessings, by the way of creation (such as destitutions - disasters and problems) and by the way of shari'ah (Islamic laws)[14] (such as performing sawm), so that when faced with shortage, people would realize that this blessing is valuable and what would happen if that blessing did not exist.

Sometimes it may occur to the mind of some unaware individuals that what would it matter if Allah arranged men's lives in such a way that no poor and oppressed person would be found in the world and the people would live in pleasure and joy without making efforts, pains-taking and enduring the suffering? It should be said that this is one of Allah's wisdoms in His planning for men, so that by this means, people would understand the various blessings and become conscious of their significance.

---

[14] Related to takwin (creation) such as destitutions, disasters and problems, and related to tashri' (divine legislation) such as sawm.

At-Tawhid: Monotheism

In a riwayat it has been said that Jibra'il (AS) came to the Holy Prophet (SA) of Islam and after conveying Allah's salutations to him said: *"O the Prophet (SA) of Allah, the Almighty Allah has sent a message to you that if you want, He will put all the treasures on earth at your disposal"*, (of course the expression of such a riwayat is for our education and understanding the significance of the matter, otherwise Allah is aware of the heart (the inner desires) of His Prophet (SA)).

The Holy prophet (SA) of Islam replied: *"I beseech Allah to feed me one day so that I will fulfill the thanks-giving to His blessings and to keep me hungry for one day so that I will well understand my needfulness, destitution and poverty towards the Almighty Allah."*[15] This is a great lesson of At-Tawhid and wisdom as to why there should occur hardships in man's life.

One of the very significant (divine) rules in planning for men is that man acquires the merit and capability for understanding and attaining divine invisible aids when he bears certain hardships and tolerates pressures. We, in the world of nature know a series of causes and effects, for instance, when our physical condition becomes ready to use foodstuffs and to assimilate them.

---

[15] "Jami'us-Sa'adat", vol. 2, p. 59.

At-Tawhid in the Value System of Islam

If one eats food while he is satiated, this food not only does not benefit him, but also afflicts him with various diseases and also spoils the food previously taken (by him) to, because his body is not in a condition to assimilate the food. But if one's stomach becomes empty and one feels hungry, then the body uses the food one eats and assimilates it. The same is also true of man's spiritual condition and man becomes fit to benefit from the divine invisible (hidden) aids and the supernatural blessings when a feeling of need and vacuum come into existence in his spirit and cuts his attention off from the causes and so long as one's attention is not cut off from the natural causes and worldly causes, he will not conceive the Divine occult blessing.

This is a very significant point which has been emphasized in many Ayat and even in our day-to-day life we need to notice this point, so that we can analyze the events (both the events related to the individual life and those related to the social area) and strengthen our faith concerning divine wisdom.

In the wars of the "Early Islam", sometimes, people's attention, due to weakness of recognition and weakness of faith, was drawn to external causes and they said: *"Thanks to Allah, everything is provided for us and there will not be any defeat for us any longer".* But at that very time, in spite of the existence of ordinary causes and conditions, they still suffered a defeat and the divine aids no longer came to their help.

> *"...And on the day of Hunayn, when your great numbers made you vain, but they availed you nothing... (9:25)."*

One of such battles was the Battle of Hunayn. In the beginning of the battle, the Muslims, due to the excess of power and war equipment, said in their hearts: *"We certainly will become victorious in this war",* but because of paying attention and relying upon external causes, they suffered defeat. But in the Battle of Badr, because they felt themselves weak, and humble, and beseeched to Allah, though they were not at all ready for fighting, yet Allah helped them and rushed to their aid:

> *"And Allah did certainly assist you at Badr when you were weak... (3:123)."*

So, this is a general rule that so long as the faithful men's attention is towards the natural causes, they will not be embraced by Allah's favors and that this divine grace will include them when they cut themselves of from everything, turn their attention solely to Allah and give up relying on material causes. Hardships, problems, disasters and discomforts are most effective in paving the ground for the realization of this condition, namely, cutting man's attention off towards anything other than Allah.

Divine Qada' (Destiny) and Qadr (Decree)

Besides these general divine planning's which are, to a large extent, understandable for the people, the particular planning are also not independent of Allah. In the Holy Qur'an it has been said that all that occurs in the world is by Allah's will and no phenomenon, in any place, is realized without Allah's will, including man's death:

"And no soul will ever die but with the permission of Allah, (at the end of) an appointed term... (3:145)."

Each man has a fixed appointed time (for life) and a decreed fate which the Allah - The Almighty has determined and his death comes when Allah's wise destination demands it. In other words, no man dies without Allah's permission and no man dies outside the time appointed by Allah and ordained in the book of his fate which has been determined by the Allah - The Almighty, be his death a natural death or an unnatural one, be it in the way of the truth or in the way of falsehood.

At-Tawhid: Monotheism

This is one of the matters which have a very constructive role in men's life. Of course, if Islamic learning's are taught properly, but however deviational expression are set forth in these fields, from the best and loftiest learning's, wrong and undesirable results will be derived and this is one of the jobs in which the Shayatin and the satanic men have invariably indulged themselves.

One of those matters which have been the object of incorrect interpretations is this very matter of predestination and men's fate. Some have thought that the Almighty Allah has predestined a fate for each man which means that man's free choice is totally not allowed towards fate and that what happens to man is outside the domain of his will-power and free-choice and that he himself can play no role in it. (this is that very fatalistic inclination which has prevailed in some of the Islamic philosophical schools and still the remnants of such thoughts are more or less existing in many of the Islamic countries and among the Muslim nations), whereas, the predestination and fate of man do not mean negating his free choice, his being answerable and responsible.

In the system of creation, we have a discussion on creation and the real courses of the world, as to what has occurred, what is occurring and what will occur in the world and there is also another part which concerns divine legislation and men's duties, what they should do and what is their responsibility towards themselves and that what effects the actions that they fulfill out of their own free will, will have on their lives in this world and in the hereafter.

Correct Clarification of the Meaning of Divine Qada' and Qadr

Unfortunately, the mixing up of these two subjects has brought about undesirable results, so much so that it has not only had no positive and constructive role on some people, but negative effects have also resulted from them. Here, we do not have the time to pay to philosophical discussion and the technical doubts in this connection and their expression and solution, and/or to survey the matter historically, i.e., to survey when and by what factors these inclinations prevailed and what effects resulted from them.

However, we can briefly say that at the time of the usurping rules when the spirit of Islam and the Islamic goals were at the utmost degree of their state of being disregarded, some of these deviated ideas, including fatalism, were projected for political private motives. The Banu Umayyah (Umayyad) rulers, for making the people obey and follow them, encouraged some persons to spread such thoughts

At-Tawhid: Monotheism

among the people that whatever happens, since Allah has willed, all should accept it and offer no resistance against it.

In this connection, there are many examples. Ibn 'Abbas (one of the Sahabah (companions of the Holy prophet (SA) of Islam) says: *"During a journey in which, we were going on a war, along with the second caliph, the caliph summoned me and said: "Do you know why your cousin (meaning 'Ali ibn Abi Talib (AS) did not take part in this war?" I replied: "I do not know." He said; "He stayed in Madinah to prepare the ground for his own khilafah (succession) after me, so that he would become khalifah (successor of Prophet Muhammad (SA)) after me." I said: "My cousin believes that he has no need for preparing such ground, because Allah's Prophet had appointed him for Khilafah." The second caliph said: "Yes! The Prophet wanted to do this! But Allah did not will it."*[16] This saying, in any way interpreted, according to what has been narrated, is a sign of a narrow-mindedness concerning Islamic learning's.

It is clear that what occurs in the world is subject to the Divine creational will. But this does not mean that it is also subject to the Divine legislative will. Allah - The Almighty, with His creational will has paid attention to all events, so that nothing happens

---

[16] "Sharhu Nahjul Balaghah", Ibn Abil-Hadid.

without His creational will. The rise of 'Sayyidush-Shuhada' Al-Imam Al-Husayn (AS) and his becoming martyred, are in accordance with the divine creational will, but this does not mean (Divine) permission for his killing and the negation of responsibility from those who took part in his martyrdom.

Likewise, those who, after the demise of the Holy prophet (SA) of Islam sat on the seat of caliphate over Muslims and who also later turned the Islamic khilafah into the form of Umayyad and Abbasid monarchy, acted as per Allah's creational will, but from the viewpoint of His legislative will, namely legitimately by no means they were permitted to commit such an act and they did not have the right to usurping deprive Islam and the Muslims from their indisputable right Therefore, it should be noticed that men are responsible for what takes place as per the divine creational will, whether in connection with the individual issues and/or in connection with the social affairs and will see their worldly and otherworldly effects.

This was a reference to a very precise subject which should be pursued in scientific circles. However, to see how man, while being possessed of free will and performing his works with free will and free choice, is under Divine planning, we will give a simple example:

'Consider two persons who come out of their homes in the morning; one aiming to go to the bakery to buy bread and the other to board a bus and go to his work, but at a road crossing they come across each other, discuss a matter with each other and take a decision for an action. For example, they decide to go to the warfront (to fight against the aggressors) or to rush to the help of homeless flood-stricken people or to fulfill another good deed and/or God-forbid, commit a sinful act. It is obvious that these two persons came out of their homes with their own free will and decided to fulfill some acts with their own free choice.

But this is not inconsistent with the belief that Allah arranges the matters in such a way that a ground be made so that the persons think of going to the warfronts out of free will. But if these two events did not occur simultaneously and one of the two persons came out of the house when the other person had already boarded the bus and left (for his work) and/or vice versa, these two persons would not meet each other and would not decide to go to the warfront together. This is an example of predestination. You see, Allah has arranged the events in such a way that good and wise consequences will result from them which will bring about perfection for Allah's creatures and open a way towards their salvation.'

Here, we quote another example which is about Prophet Musa (Moses) (AS) from the Holy Qur'an, When Musa (AS) reached maturity under the care of Fir'awn (Pharaoh) and killed a Coptic (Egyptian) man, a person guided him, saying that he should leave the place, because the men of Fir'awn were attempting a plot on his (Musa's) life. Musa (AS), too, took his advice, left Egypt and went towards Madyan.

After going through a long way, he reached the vicinity of Madyan. There the people had gathered over a well and were drawing water out of it to water their sheep. Musa (AS), tired and hungry, had sat down on a corner to get over his fatigue when suddenly his eyes fell on two chaste girls who were standing in a corner and keeping their sheep there. Musa (AS) got up, went to them and asked: *"Why do you water your sheep?"*

They replied: *"We have an aged father who is staying at home and who is unable to fulfill the pastoral deeds. So, we have to bring the sheep here ourselves, so that after the shepherds water their sheep, we will water our sheep and/or somebody will help us and draw a*

At-Tawhid: Monotheism

bucket of water out of the well and we water our sheep. We cannot do it on our own."

Musa (AS) came forward, took the bucket and watered the sheep ... and, the story continues, as we know, from Surah 28 of the Holy Qur'an, and Prophet Shu'ayb (Jethro) (AS) married one of his daughters to Musa (AS) and Musa (AS) spent ten years in Madyan serving as a shepherd for Shu'ayb (AS).

All these events which constitute a system of miscellaneous phenomena are the actions which certain persons, out of their own free-will have fulfilled out of particular motives and for specified goals. Musa (AS) did not leave Egypt aiming to come to Prophet Shu'ayb (AS). He wanted to be saved from the mischief of Fir'awn and probably he apparently did not know that Shu'ayb (AS) was there, and that he had a daughter and that in that city he was the Prophet.

But Allah had predestined that on one hand, Musa (AS) comes to the service of a great Prophet (AS) such as Prophet Shu'ayb (AS), who because of his old-age was lacking the ability to work, and to fulfill his duties towards the others. (He had) predestined that Shu'ayb (AS)'s daughter marries Musa (AS) and that after ten years, when Musa (AS) was appointed a Prophet (by Allah), they return to Egypt and call upon Fir'awn to worship the One God - Allah -The One and Only. These were all Allah's predestinations.

However, in any place of these predestinations, did any compulsion exist over Musa (AS), Shu'ayb (AS) or his daughter? No! The actions were all out of free-choice. Yet, there is a wise arrangement and plan over all these planning's and that is Allah's planning. It is here that Allah says: *"O Musa You came here on the basis of an exact deliberation and precise plan and these events should have happened so that in this safe valley you will receive the divine Prophetic mission and go to Fir'awn."* Those (events) were preliminaries for this task, but in no stage did they cause any compulsion over Musa (AS) or the others.

If one carefully thinks about the events in his daily life, he will see that in each phenomenon, there are thousands of preliminaries which Allah - The Almighty has provided with His planning device and that we are neglectful of the fact that what wise planning rules over each and every one of the events of the world.

One of the great men of religion (may Allah be please with him) said: *"If a man thinks about the secrets of his life and if he has (inwardly) clear-sighted eyes and a conscious heart, he will see as if the whole world has been created for him and that all things are preliminaries for him so that his affairs will he performed in a perfect way."*

Likewise, if another man thinks in this way, he will reach the same result. In a hadithun-qudsiyy (a hadith which relates a revelation from Allah in the language of the Prophet (SA)) Allah - The Almighty says: *"I treat each one of the off springs of Adam so kindly and compassionately as if I had just that very creature, but My creatures treat Me as if everybody but Me were their God."*

This is a complaint from Allah in this hudithun-qudsiyy and so, each creature should know that he is constantly under the planning and supervision of Allah and that what Allah ordains for him alongside with having responsibility is good and is a duty for him. Therefore, we should know that the divine pre-destinations are all to our advantage, even if they are from disasters and hardships and apparently to our disadvantage.

If a child falls sick at home and his affectionate mother prevents him from eating some kinds of food and/or even for his rapid recovery makes him take bitter medicines and takes him for injections, she is certainly meaning good for him and these actions (of the mother) are the very signs of her kindness and affection, thought the child might be displeased with this behavior of the mother and accuse her of mercilessness. Therefore, the existence of bitter and annoying events (including floods and earthquakes) are not aimless and are under the wise planning of Allah, though the actions are fulfilled as per the individuals' free choice, too, and that the sinners are also responsible for their indecent actions. The Holy Qur'an says:

"No evil befalls on the earth nor in your own souls, but it is in a book before We bring it into existence; surely that is easy for Allah; So that you may not grieve for what has escaped you, nor be exultant at what He has given you; and Allah does not love any arrogant boaster (57:22-23)."

No disaster befalls anybody unless it has been written in a book before and this (as everything else) is easy for Allah to do. Then, immediately Allah expresses the reason for this: so that you believe in Allah's wise planning and should not be worried if anything is lost by you; if you lose any properly, if a house is ruined, if a dear one is martyred and you should know that this is divine pre-destination. And on the other hand, so that you do not become proud and arrogantly gay either when the joys turn to you, and that you will always notice the fact that you are dutiful and responsible in the face of each and every event, whether pleasant of unpleasant and that you should only be thinking of fulfilling your duties.

The Imam of the ummah (Imam Khumayni (QS)) had, from the very years of 1341 SH and 1342 SH (solar hijrah) (1962 and 1963 AD) repeatedly said: *"We aim at the fulfillment of our duties and do not mind what happens. If we fight, it is not known to us that we will be one hundred per cent victorious. But when our duty is to fight, we fight, even though we apparently suffer a defeat."*

In some of the battles of the early Islam, such as the Battle of Uhud, too, Muslims suffered defeat, but because they fought for the fulfillment of their duty and the exaltation of the word of At-Tawhid in the world, they were always satisfied and their faith in the leadership of the Holy Prophet (SA) of Islam never decreased either. They said:

"Say: Nothing will afflict us save what Allah has ordained for us; He is our Patron; and on Allah let the believers rely (9:51)."

The logic of these believers was that what Allah has predestined for us will happen and that we arc contented with His predestination, though they might be unpleasant. Many of the events are not pleasing for us and hurt our sentiments, but we must know that Allah's wise planning is above these and that, as a whole, these phenomena will be useful for the progress of Islam and the fulfillment of the Islamic movement. Therefore, we should fulfill our own duties and seek the true goodness which is achieved just in the light of the fulfillment of our religious duties. As fur what happens, it does not concern us. The universe has a Creator and a Planner Who has left nobody to himself, He knows what should happen and what is expedient.

The phenomena of this world are from one aspect a combination of good and evil, pleasant and unpleasant. Sometimes there is good health and sometimes there is illness; in one year there is security and comfort and in the other year insecurity and suffering, but none are absolute good and evil. True good and evil depend on how man faces that phenomenon.

All of us regard health to be good. But if one abuses good health and falls into committing sin, is good health still to his good? Would it not be closer to his good and felicity if he were ill and could not commit that sin? Property, wealth and welfare are not always good for man either, and it depends on how man treats them.

Of course, from the view point that Allah has created all, all are good, but their being good and evil for you and I depend on the manner in which we treat them. The Almighty Allah, plans the world affairs such that men can derive various benefits from these double-faced phenomena and stand by the promise they have made with Allah that they will help His religion to the last drop of their blood, so that they will attain both the glory, honor and victory of this world and the eternal felicity and mercy.

Part 2: At-Tawhid in the Ideological System of Islam

In the Name of Allāh, the Most Gracious, the Most Merciful

The second part of this subject concerns At-Tawhid in the value system of Islam. The terms "value", "value system" and other words of this kind are quite prevalent in today's terminology and people have become familiar with these terms. But since this term "value" has in fact been translated from other languages and has gone into our culture and is not from the viewpoint of concept and contents which are in conformity with the interpretations and words which have appeared in the genuine culture of Islam and the riwayat, it is necessary to first give an explanation about this term giving an extensive meaning which is today meant by it, so that we are able to see what equivalent of this term is in the Islamic culture.

The Concept of Value

The common and general concept which we have about the term "value" is in fact the economic concept. The relation of a commodity and/or a service with the thing man is ready to pay for getting that commodity or service brings into existence the concept of value. But the meaning of value and the value system is other than this economic concept, though it is not totally alien to this concept and though it might very probably have at first been harrowed from this very economic concept.

The justification which can be made is that we are ready to pay some money for a good and/or a service or to deliver another good or service in return for that when that good and/or service are desired and liked by us and we have a liking for them. A hungry man needs food. Food is desirable for him and he is ready to pay some money in return, which satisfies his need. So, the criterion for economic value too, is in fact desirability and being demanded.

Hence we can abstract this meaning from its economic specifications and say: *"anything which is desired and demanded by man and which can meet his need or his want, that thing is of value."* The term "value", in this extensive meaning is both applied to objects as well as to men and their conduct. But since our discussion is about man and his behavior, we have to continue speaking in this connection. Now let us see which man is more valuable from the viewpoint of Islam.

Man's Honor

In spite of what is propounded in today's world culture and which is also claimed by the humanists that each man, due to his being a human, has a natural value and in other words has honor, even though he might commit many murders and crimes Islam considers two kinds of honor for man.

The first kind is general honor, meaning that each man, due to his being a man (irrespective of his conducts and attitudes) enjoys that honor. This is a creational honor and a God-given value which the Almighty Allah has bestowed upon man and which He has not bestowed upon the other creatures and perhaps the axis of these God-given blessings is man's intellect. In some of the ayat of the Holy Qur'an, too, this creational honor has been pointed out:

"And surely We have honored the children of Adam, and We carry them in the land and the sea, and We have given them of the good things, and We have made them to excel by an appropriate excellence over most of those whom We have created (17:70)."

In the above ayah of the Holy Qur'an, it has been stipulated that Allah has bestowed an honor to the children of Adam (AS) and excelled them to many of His creatures. This honoring includes all men, namely, both man and woman, little and mature possess the human creational specifications. Allah has given them eyes, ears and the other limbs and parts (of the body), a beautiful and erect body, and has also bestowed upon them mind, intellect, intelligence, talents and the other spiritual and physical characteristics which every man enjoys.

But when we meditate, we will see that this honor and value in reality belong to Allah and that it is He Who has bestowed these blessings on men freely and that men have themselves no role in attaining this honor.

The other kind of honor is that which man himself with free -will and the power of free choice and free selection which the Almighty Allah has granted him achieves and attains. In this kind of honor, not all men are equal and it is enjoyed just by the virtuous and if some men act un-virtuously, they will not only have any share of this honor, but rather they will get anti-value and fall so down that they will become lower than any animal. About this group of men who have not acquired any honor for themselves the Holy Qur'an says:

"...They are as cattle, nay, they are in worse errors; these are the heedless ones (7:179)."

Hence, that creational honor does not suffice for man to become recognized as an honorable and noble creature forever, because he may lose the God-given honor and buy for himself anti-honor, namely, meanness and lowness. The expression of the Holy Qur'an in this regard is such:

> "Certainly We created man in the best make. Then We render him the lowest of the low (95:4-5)."

Allah has created man in the best and most admirable form and fulfilled His creational honoring in the best manner, but some men are found who deprive themselves from this divine honor and who degrade themselves down to the lowest stages which are possible for a human being. Therefore, although all men have the creational and God-given honor in common, but in the stage of free choice all are not the same and equal and will have different degrees of value and honor in proportion to the difference in their degrees of virtuousness, and even sometimes some may degrade themselves so much that no honor is viewed for them and they should be omitted from the society like cancerous glands.

Moral Value

The other matter which concerns this subject is men's conduct which generally constitutes the main axis or our discussion in this series of matters. Here, starts the display of arts among the philosophers of law, the philosophers of ethics and the various thinkers of humanity. However, during tens of centuries in which they have discussed about these subjects, still their thought has not reached any decisive and correct result. A short introduction will serve to open the way towards this discussion, paying attention to which helps us in attaining this objective.

Basically, any free action fulfilled by a free agent is for the sake of attaining the result which is derived from that action and very often it might be that no action would take place if no goal was in view.

Therefore, since every action is a means for a goal, and no action is in itself desirable by nature, the value and desirability or every action is also subject to the result which is derived from that action.

The person who intends to go on a trip, takes a series of actions, for instance, he buys tickets, prepares the means and necessities for the trip and gets ready for boarding the bus or an aero plane. But by fulfilling these preliminary actions he certainly means to reach the goal, the destination and the place he has in view, and does not mean the mere fulfillment of these actions.

Here, there is a very delicate point of which many of those involved in discussion and reasoning arc neglectful and it is that sometimes some results are derived from one's actions which either he does not know and/or does not notice, or for which he has not fulfilled that action.

For instance, when one leaves home to go to visit his friend or to go to school or to perform some other action, if en route, other results follow this action of his which (results) he has not considered at all, nor he has meant them, it cannot be said that he has fulfilled this action for that result (which he had not meant). So, the value of man's free action is subject to the result which he has meant from the beginning and which he has put as his goal.

Another example will serve to better clarify this matter; a person builds a hospital for showing off and so that the people will applaud him and his only goal in spending money and time is gaining fame and popularity among the people. Now if this hospital is built and thousands of people, including the esteemed Islamic combatants and the fighters in the way of Allah are treated in that hospital, and good result is derived from this action, can it be said that the builder of the hospital (the person referred to) will also derive a benefit from this action? Certainly not! Because his aim has not been the realization of these results and only the love for fame has driven him to perform such an action.

On the contrary, if a person builds a hospital with the intention that Allah's creatures and the wounded and the oppressed people of the society use it, but a bomb happens to hit and destroy that hospital and so the building of the hospital would not lead to any result, his action has by no means-become valueless, because he had indeed built the hospital for an invaluable goal. Of course if that hospital remained safe and the aims of construction were also fulfilled, he would achieve more benefits.

The Criterion for Moral Value

Now, taking into consideration the above introductions which clarify that besides the result's being taken into consideration, intention and viewing the aim have also direct hearing on giving value to man's actions, the question is raised as to what behavior men should have and what goal they should take into consideration so that their actions, conducts and behaviors become valuable? Before paying attention to this matter, we should first see what is basically the truth and criterion for values from the viewpoint of Islam?

As a whole, the truth and criterion for values from the viewpoint of Islam and the value system of this school (the school of Islam) is that perfection which emerges in man's soul and which leads man towards worshiping Allah, getting near to Him and winning

His favor. This perfection is not a conventional concept and is like physical power, a reality and a fact. Of course this perfection is to be achieved as a result of the free actions of men themselves so it will become possessed of moral value and the man possessing perfection attains true honor and real nobility.

Therefore, from the viewpoint of Islam, only the acquired spiritual perfections are the source of the exalted and positive human value, otherwise physical and body perfections have no genuine value and even the God-given powers of the soul cannot by themselves be the source of value either.

Extraordinary intelligence and strong memory do not by themselves become the source of the perfection of the soul, because there have been persons who were endowed with high-level of intelligence but who however sank into the lowest abysses of human fall and/or who misused their intelligence and intellect for selling out themselves and the others. So, intelligence by itself is not a source of absolute value.

Intelligence and memory are not absolute values; rather they are rated as tools for attaining true values.

At-Tawhid: Monotheism

People, more or less, measure some of the values with their own innate nature and intellect, included among such values are truthfulness, honesty and standing by one's words. But sometimes the matter reaches such a stage, the reality of which cannot be understood by all and rather the superior ones (those who are above the others in respect of spiritual perfection and knowledge of the religion) should understand it and teach it to the others and even, more significant than this, some of the values are not recognizable with man's ordinary thought. It is there that wahy rushes to the help of man and makes those values recognizable. Many of the moral and legal issues in the value system of Islam are determined just on the basis of wahy and their limits, terms and details are defined by the Divine Law.

For example, we briefly know that if we tell a lie which causes an innocent person to be released from the hands of an oppressor, such a lie does not have the indecency the other lies have, but how far and with what conditions? These are the issues to be determined by the Divine law. So, the basis of values consists of the virtues, qualities and manners which exalt and perfect man's soul. Among the values which are propounded in various communities of the world, there are matters which all people have- more or less accepted but which they are unable to understand.

All know that justice is good. But what is the criterion for this goodness'? All know that truthfulness and honesty are good. But which truthfulness and which honesty'? All know that the spirit of self-sacrifice is beautiful, but by what criterion? If we acquire these criteria properly, we can judge in cases of doubt and mistake properly. For example, today, in all world communities, freedom is propounded as a great value, so that if anyone says: *I oppose freedom;* it is as if he has said that I oppose the light of the sun. But do all know as to what is the criterion for this value?

The Value of Freedom

The word "freedom" has a very broad concept and has different meanings. Certainly it cannot, with this extent, be a criterion for value and the reason for making mistakes and misusing these concepts is this very fact that these values have been spread without acquiring their criterion and that the people, too, have accepted them for the sake of their sensual desires.

Anyhow, the desirability of freedom is not absolute. Rather, it is a means and tools for that spiritual perfection which is attained as a result of the person's free will and free choice. Suppose that if we leave a child free in a house where the child is surrounded by explosives or poisonous medicines, the child can freely light the match and approach the gas capsule and/or can throw the lit match near a vessel of gasoline or can consume a poisonous medicine, have we (by doing so) caused the child to become perfected or have we caused it to be killed?

Is, from the viewpoint of logic and intellect, giving such freedom to the child correct? Or, should the child be left free to the extent that it does not harm itself and the others? Of course, if we tie up the child's hands and legs or confine it to a cage, it will never make human growth.

The child should be left free, but within a specified and planned framework and should not be left totally free. When this child reaches maturity and distinguishes between good and bad, then he should be left free. Also human individuals in different societies have different degrees of wisdom, perfection and recognition. If the general people (in a society) are not perfectly aware and the means for any kind of action is at their disposal, its result will be nothing but destruction for that people.

It is not proper on the strength of the fact that freedom is an absolute value, to make all things for all individuals free so that they will behave in any way they choose. This is a wrong logic. This is of the inauspicious souvenirs of the Western culture which has spread in our society. We should know these anti-values and separate them from the true values so that we can bring our society near to more and more growth on the basis of the Islamic values and attain that perfection which, if not achieved by man, can be replaced by nothing else.

Commitment and Sense of Duty

We have already mentioned that value is sometimes applied to man's free conduct (the actions he performs out of free -will) and it is said that such and such an action is valuable and this term "value" is sometimes applied to the final goal of these conducts and it is expressed that for what values) such and such actions are performed.

In other words, in a value system, firstly we should take into view a final goal so that for attaining that final goal the actions become valuable, provided that that very goal itself has innate and genuine value, and secondly we choose such conducts that are commensurate with that value. The most general and universal valuable conduct which exists in all value systems (whether or not those who propound that system are heedful of that general value) is commitment and being bound to fulfill the duties and responsibilities.

In the midst of such kinds of systems which are propounded in the world, one of the European moral philosophers named Kant notices this point and says: "*A good action is that which is fulfilled for the sake of the fulfillment of duty.*" He has properly understood this far that a general value for all actions and conducts is the fulfillment of the duty. But what has been away from his view and has remained undone (in his expressions) is that the fulfillment of the duty itself is not the final end, rather its value is for the sake of another genuine and innate value, named man's "final perfection" which is attained in the light of proximity to Allah.

The word "committed' which is used in today's public culture, is applied to the one who attempts to know his duty and fulfill it. But in Islam, we have by far a richer and more meaningful term than the terms.

"commitment" and "being bound over" and that is the beautiful term "taqwa" (piety). Taqwa is that very commitment which is propounded in other moral systems, plus the particular specifications which have arisen out of the Islamic attitude and culture. Although there have been detailed discussions about the concept of taqwa and basically in all sermons of the salatul-Jumu'ah (Friday prayer), it (taqwa) should be enjoined and emphasized, however, as it suits the matter, we shall express a few points briefly in this connection so far as it concerns the discussion.

Taqwa

The term "taqwa" which is from the root "wiqayah" and which means "guarding" is applied where something which is exposed to danger and corruption is to be guarded. This is the literal meaning of "wiqayah" and also "taqwa" which is the infinitive mood and/or the verbal noun of "ittiqa" that contains this same meaning. But "taqwa", as a moral concept, has a particular point and that is that man feels that as a result of some conducts, the perfection and purity of his soul and the value of his being are endangered.

Here, two basic points exist which separate the moral taqwa from its other meanings, the first point is that what is in danger is man's soul, not his body and physique and the second point is that the danger which threatens a man's soul, is his own conduct, not the other men's conduct, nor the natural events.

So, it is appropriate that man behaves in such a way as to remain guarded so that his soul will not be contaminated, will not fall in respect of value, will not be fallen and declined and will not be afflicted with eternal torment. In such cases man has naturally also fear of contamination or danger, because if he does not have fear, he will not attempt to guard himself. That is why in the concept of taqwa, the concept of fear has also been guaranteed and the expressions of the Holy Qur'an and the riwayat and the case of common usage, indicate that this is the case:

"And be on your guard against a day when one soul shall not avail another in the least... (2:48,123)."

Fear the day when no one comes to the help of another one and for such fearing, guard yourselves from such danger (both the meaning of guarding and the meaning of fear are considered.).

In the Islamic attitude which is based on At-Tawhid (monotheistic) viewpoint, we know all effects to be from Allah. Although there exist causes and means for these effects, but eventually it is Allah Who moves the chain of the world of being, Who is the cause of all causes and Who is the Maker of all means. Therefore, on the basis of At-Tawhid in actions if a danger threatens a person, it is also in the control of Allah.

So, if a person fears lest in future his existence, his life, his perfection and purity and also his honor and nobility be endangered, from the At-Tawhid outlook (the outlook based on At-Tawhid), he fears lest Allah -The Almighty should provide the means so that he will fall, whether in worldly means or the means of the hereafter. So this fear eventually leads to fear of Allah and so if we fear lest we should fall, we should fear Allah, i.e., lest Allah should let us fall, or if we fear lest our soul should be polluted or lest we should become afflicted with eternal torment and remoteness from Allah's mercy, we should fear Allah and regard Him as the Maker of all causes and this attitude becomes the cause and source for taqwa to be attached to Allah -The Almighty in the Islamic culture.

Do meditate about the ayat of the Holy Qur'an,

> "O you who believe! Be careful of (your duty to) Allah... (59:18)."

The word "ittaqu" means be careful, guard yourself, but what role does the word "Allah" have here? "Allah" is the object of the verb "ittaqu", it means fear Allah and guard yourselves against that danger which threatens you from Allah as punishment for the (bad) actions you do out of free choice.

So, it became clear that taqwa is that very commitment towards the fulfillment of the duties with richer and more fruitful concepts. That is to say, in the concept of taqwa, both the spiritual source of taqwa which consists of fear of danger and the fact that the effects and emergence of these dangers and falls are in Allah's hands have been noticed. It is He Who can make this danger reach man, Who can descend torment upon him or keep him secure from those dangers. and since the man's fall in the hereafter is the torment in hell, sometimes fire and torment have been regarded as pertaining to taqwa:

"...Then fear the fire whose fuel is people and stones... (2:24)."

The like of the above ayah has also been employed from the root word "wiqayah":

"...Save yourselves and your families from a fire... (66:6)."

The word "qu" (save) is from that very root word "wiqayah". So, sometimes taqwa is attributed to the fire, torment and hell, due to the fact that it (taqwa) is the means which hinders man from fall. Also, on some occasions, taqwa is attributed to a time:

"And be on your guard against a day when one soul shall not avail another in the least... (2:48, 123)."

Fear the day when no one rushes to the help of the other and no one suffices another one's cause. That day is the Qiyamah (Resurrection Day). Another point which should be taken into view in taqwa is that sometimes taqwa is regarded as the adjective of the verb itself and its application is meant to enjoin performing the prayers (and other religious duties) and to desist from the sins and sometimes too it is applied just to desist from the sins:

"No (good) action, if coupled with taqwa is little."[17]

In the above riwayat, good action has been placed alongside taqwa, namely, fulfill good actions and do not commit sins. So, according to one probability, by taqwa in the above riwayat it is meant that if you want your good actions to be useful, you should also desist from bad actions, otherwise the bad actions cause the effects of the good actions to be destroyed, too. For example, if you collect money in a bag, but however because there is a hole in the bottom of the bag, though you have worked and taken trouble too, you have saved nothing.

---

[17] Al-'Usul al-Kafi, vol. 2, p. 75.

According to a ruwayah, the Holy Prophet (SA) of Islam said to his companions: "The one who utters At- Tasbihatul-Arba'ah (the four praises): 'subhanallalhi wal-hamdu lillahi wa la ilahaillallahu wallahu akbar', for each praise Allah grows a tree in Paradise for him." One of the Companions of the prophet (SA) remarked: "O the Prophet (SA) of Allah! So, we have plenty of trees in Paradise." The Holy Prophet (SA) of Islam replied: "If you do not send a fire to burn the trees." Good actions bear (good) fruits if they are accompanied by taqwa, namely, by desisting from sins.

Therefore, one of the cases of the application of taqwa is the very desisting from sins and its other application consists of that spiritual state which becomes the source of the fulfillment of duties and desisting from forbidden acts. Also, sometimes taqwa is applied to that state of fear which becomes the origin of this action and eventually another case of the application of taqwa is a spiritual Slate which is realized in man's soul.

This fixed spiritual quality which is called the well-grounded quality, is a fixed spiritual slate which is present in man's soul and which is not quickly given up. Those who during years of assiduity and practice, have acted according to their duties, a well-grounded quality develops in them so that automatically, anywhere a duty is to be performed, they immediately act.

In a broader definition and explanation it should be expressed that man's spiritual states are divided into two groups; one group consists of transient, changeable and unstable states which states, in the philosophical terminology is interpreted as "hal" (natural disposition) and the other group consists of permanent, stable and well-grounded qualities in the soul which is interpreted as "malakuh" (fixed spiritual quality).

These states and qualities are propounded in the case of all the value behaviors of man. Chastity, modesty, self-sacrifice and the like, arc sometimes in the form of a transient state and sometimes in the form of a constant spiritual quality and it exists in the form of a malakah in the soul.

In the traditional and classical ethics, the discussion is on malakat, namely, those constant and firm qualities which exist in individuals' souls, but in value concepts in the general meaning, individual and personal behaviors which stern from transient states should also be discussed.

That is, for the clarification of the value system of a school (of thought) it does not suffice that we just rely on the malakat, because eventually the question may arise as to what value does this behavior, which has not reached the level of malakah, has from the viewpoint of this system. Is it totally lacking in value? Certainly this is by no means the case.

So, the value of behaviors should also be discussed irrespective of malakat. Consider a youth who has just reached maturity (from the point of view of the religious duties). When he performs his actions with a divine motive, his deed is taqwa, even though malakah may not yet have come into existence in him.

The expressions of the Holy Qur'an and the Infallible Imams (SA) too are mostly viewing the behavior and do not mean that one should necessarily have the malakah of taqwa, Because if a person religiously becomes mature just today, he is duty-bound to have taqwa.

Besides all these, basically the malakat, from two aspects, have direct and close relationship with actions and conducts, one that they (malakat) are themselves caused by behaviors, namely, they come into existence as a result of practice, assiduity and continued action and on the other hand, they are the cause of further actions. Therefore, taqwa, in the meaning of an abstract title conforms to actions, not just malakah and that spiritual quality which is discussed in ethics.

The other matter which should not be neglected in regard to taqwa is that when we say that in the value system of Islam no good action is outside taqwa, this imagination should not occur that just physical and perceptible action is meant; rather by action, it is meant here as a philosophical concept, that is, any kind of activity which stems from man's soul, whether it is in man's heart and the environment of the mind, or outside the body and on external matters, whether it be a physical action or a spiritual action.

When you are seated, your body is not in movement and you are not bringing about changes in external matters, but with thinking and meditating, you can fulfill an action which has value and which is rewarded in the hereafter or vice-versa, i.e., an action which is among severe and cardinal sins, such as unduly suspecting your faithful brothers.

Sometimes even refraining from an action becomes the proof of taqwa. Suppose a youth faces a situation which tempts the commitment of a sin, but he controls himself and does not commit that sin.

Here, apparently no action has been fulfilled, but in reality a great action has taken place and that is deciding to desist from the sin and in the terminology of fuqaha (the Islamic jurisprudents), it is kaffun-nafs (controlling one's self), that is, a spiritual energy should be spent so that man can restrain himself from committing a sin.

Hence, taqwa includes the palpable, external and physical actions as well as the spiritual actions and even desisting from (sinful) actions, when it is with decision and out of consciousness. But if desisting from a sinful action is unconsciously and without intention, such as when a man is asleep and in this state no sin is committed by him, such a person has (in that condition) desisted from sin(s), but his action is not taqwa, rather it is utter negation and there is no a affirmative aspect, nor spiritual activity in it, because neither spiritual energy has been spent, nor any decision has been taken for anything. So, those who imagine that taqwa is just desisting from sin(s) and thus keep aloof from the community so that no error and sin might be committed by them have in fact performed no action and arc not muttaqi (possessed of taqwa, virtuous, pious). Taqwa requires spiritual activity.18

---

18 It has even been narrated that in the past some unaware persons had blinded or had closed their eyes so that they couldn't look at anything haram (forbidden by Islam).

We give another example: In a scene of wrestling, two persons are busy wrestling at a gymnasium and around the scene; there are a number of spectators watching them. After some time of struggle, one of the two wrestlers falls on ground and as wrestlers call it becomes knocked down and the other wrestler who has not been knocked down will be declared as the winner. Well, as for those spectators who are seated around the scene and who have not been knocked down and who are also seated or standing erect, are they winners too?

The answer is quite clear. They have not taken part in this event so that a case for winning and losing would come forth. Taqwa is when a man draws sword against Satan and against one's soul and succeeds to guard himself from evil and commit no sins. Taqwa is an affirmative action and a positive activity, be it in one's soul or in his body. Of course the physical actions after all stem from spiritual activity and arise out of will-power and determination.

Stages of Taqwa

The other point which concerns Taqwa is that Taqwa has certain stages and it is not such that we could say it exists or it does not exist. Rather it is a matter with stages and these stages arc innumerable

At-Tawhid: Monotheism

and have no definite limits and extents either. In the ayah of the Holy Qur'an,

> "...Surely the most honorable of you with Allah is the one among you most careful (of his duty)... (49:13)."

The word (atqa), meaning the most honorable is in the superlative degree. This meaning is applied in a case where one thing has different stages, being little or in excess and/or intensity and weakness. For example, the one who performs the (obligatory) prayers so that he will be immune from Allah's torment and would not go to hell, has attained one degree of taqwa and relation with Allah, but this is a low stage and a weak relation.

A better stage and a stronger relationship with Allah belongs to the one who performs the wajib salawat not only for the sake of immunity from Allah's retribution, but also because he wishes to enter the sphere of Allah's mercy and to enjoy His eternal blessings.

Such a person, besides performing the wajib (obligatory) salawat is also attentive of the mustahab (recommended but not obligatory) salawat and tries to perform more and more mustahab acts. The loftiest stage and degree belongs to the awliya' (Allah's friends), that is, even if they know that in spite of fulfilling this religious obligation (the salawat), still Allah will take them to Hell, but He is pleased with them, they still recite salawat in order to acquire Allah's pleasure and love.

The same is also the case (with them), if they know that even there is no hell and paradise. In some supplications of the Infallible Imams (AS), it has appeared that they say (to Allah): *"O Allah! If you take me to hell and burn me for thousands of years, your love will not come out of my heart and if I know that your pleasure is, that I burn in the fire of Hell for ever, that fire will be desirable for me."*

Of course this supposition (that Allah might take the Infallible Imams (AS) to hell...) is contrary to the truth and there is no room for the probability of such a thing, but this is the spiritual state of such persons (The Infallible Imams (AS) and all other Allah's friends).

They do not demand paradise and hell and seek only Allah's meeting and pleasure. The following words are well-known from Amirul-Mu'mineen (The Commander of the Faithful) Al-Imam 'Ali (AS) who says: *"O Allah! I do not worship You out of fear of torment and desire for paradise, rather I worship You*

At-Tawhid: Monotheism

because you are lovable and worthy of being worshiped."

Anyhow, taqwa has different stages and naturally, that nearness to Allah (pleasing Allah, winning Allah's favor) which is attained due to taqwa will have different degrees. Examples of that too, sometimes in our time, are witnessed in the combatant brothers and in their last wills. Sometimes they write and sometimes it comes to their tongue that: *"O Allah, we have not come to the warfront to be rewarded with Al-hurul-'in (the pure beautiful mates in paradise), we have not come fur jihad to just be released of the torment of hell, rather since we love You and seek Your pleasure and meeting, we sacrifice our unworthy lives."*

The above points were a brief description about the concepts which are propounded about taqwa and this word by itself denotes all these delicate and precise concepts and hence it becomes clear why in the Islamic culture this word (taqwa) has been so much emphasized:

So, taking in to consideration the ayah of the Holy Qur'an,

At-Tawhid in the Ideological System of Islam

> *"...Surely the most honorable of you with Allah is the one among you most careful (of his duty)... (49:13)."*

it becomes quite clear that the most general and overall value regarding moral (permanent) dispositions and behavior is taqwa and any other thing which has value will be one of the proofs of taqwa, If justice and seeking the truth have value, it is because they arc of the proofs of taqwa. If the acquisition of knowledge is of value, it is because in the Islamic culture, it is regarded as one of the proofs of taqwa; likewise, the other values, such as self-sacrifice.

The Relationship of Taqwa with At-Tawhid

As for the relationship of taqwa with At-Tawhid, what is of significance and should he paid attention to, is that in the value system of Islam, taqwa, without relationship with Allah has no value and it is directly or indirectly related to Allah. Even this it is said:

> *"...Then fear the fire... (2:24)."*

The fire is to be feared because it is "Allah's torment"; or

> *"And guard yourselves against a day... (2:281)."*

The qiyamah (resurrection day), too, is to be guarded against because it is the day of Allah's judgment and the day of Allah's reward and punishment and taqwa becomes related and associated with it. In other words, since taqwa includes fear and the fear desired in Islam is the fear of Allah, so this concept includes a relationship with Allah and so long as we do not know Allah and do not know Him as the Possessor of all perfections and powers, no room will be found for having taqwa towards Him (for fearing Him).

The more significant relationship which At-Tawhid has with taqwa is from the viewpoint of acquiring taqwa, in the way that when we learned that taqwa is a general value and the malakah of taqwa is one of the most excellent malakat with which man is related, we should know how this malakah is acquired. One general way common to all malakat is practice, that is, anyone who wants to acquire a permanent spiritual disposition should practice and repeat the actions related to it so that that malakah will emerge out of him.

As for the malakah of taqwa (so that it will emerge in mu'minin as a permanent spiritual disposition and lifts them to the most excellent of values), the main condition is paying attention to Allah, in the way that the greater man's attention is to Allah, the better he is able to fulfill his duties and provide the ground for the emergence of malakah of taqwa in his soul.

It is true that many people perform some actions without paying attention to Allah or desist from some actions, but these kinds of conducts are not the source of that value attached to taqwa which is propounded in Islam. These provide a ground for perfection and have imperfect causality. This cause reaches its true effect and acquires perfect causality when it has a relationship with Allah, then it can be regarded as a means for man's getting near to Allah, winning Allah's pleasure and favor and for his eventual perfection and be fulfilled for the sake of its very being a means (towards winning Allah's pleasure), not out of other motives.

Suppose in a society in which theft and treachery is regarded indecent, a person avoids committing theft so that his social value will not decrease or his reputation will not be damaged, such a person has desisted from a sin, but never attains that value which is propounded in the Islamic taqwa, because a voluntary action has value when it is fulfilled for the sake of that eventual desired goal behind it. If desisting from sin is for the sake of Allah, it has that eventual value, but if it is because of fear of the people and fear of legal torment and persecution, it will no longer have that value. So, all value action of ours should be in relation to Allah and take place for the sake of getting near to Allah, winning His pleasure, favor and mercy and immunity from His torment.

In the following ayah of the Holy Qur'an,

"O you who believe! fear Allah, and let every soul consider what it has sent on for the morrow, and fear Allah; surely Allah is Aware of what you do. And be not like those who forsook Allah, so He made them forsake their own souls: these it is that are the transgressors (59:18-19)."

These two basic points have been mentioned for the acquisition of taqwa; one to be attentive to the fact that the Almighty Allah is always present and conscious and that we are in His presence and the other is that the Almighty Allah spares the reward and the punishment for no action and that He returns the result of all our actions to ourselves. Paying attention to these matters causes man to, with the fulfillment of the duties, attain divine taqwa.

The point which is contrary to taqwa, namely, that which is propounded as anti-value, is fisq (evil-doing) and fur (wickedness or debauchery); and fasiq (evil-doer) and fajir (the debauchee) is the one who does not reck any danger (neither apparent and material dangers nor the dangers which damage his humanity), and accepts no border for his own life and who, waywardly and licentiously moves in any direction he chooses to. Although, in the Holy Qur'an, taqwa is sometimes applied in the face of fur and sometimes in the face of fisq, but its proof is the same.

"And the soul and Him Who made it perfect, then He inspired it to understand what is right and wrong for it (91:7-8)."

and/or:

"...Or shall We make those who guard (against evil) like the wicked? (38:28)."

In the above ayat of the Holy Qur'an, taqwa has been propounded as a general value and fur has been propounded as an anti-value. The same is true of the ayah mentioned before.

And be not like those who forsook Allah, so He made them forsake their own souls: these it is that are the transgressors (59:19)."

These verses first emphasize taqwa:

"O you who believe! fear Allah, and let every soul consider what it has sent on for the morrow, and fear Allah; surely Allah is Aware of what you do (59:18)."

Then, it (the Holy Qur'an) mentions the point opposite to it:

"...These it is that are the transgressors (59:19)."

The term fur, in the root of the word, means impudicity and license and fisq, as the etymologists have mentioned is that something comes out of its natural shell, for example, if a date comes out of its natural shell, about it is said: "fisquttamr", Also man's existence has been surrounded by a natural border which is called the border of 'ubudiyyah' (worship to Allah).

If man comes out of this shell and transgresses that limit which Allah has ordained for him, he has committed fisq, just as taqwa is the observance of that very natural and godly border. Anyhow, the most general concept of value which has positive value is taqwa, and the most general anti-value or concept which has negative value is fisq and fur.

Ibadah (Worship to Allah)

One of the other value concepts of Islam, which is particular to the (monotheistic and godly cultures and communities, is worshiping Allah and serving Him, for, all world communities more or less accept the concept of taqwa, yet they consider its proofs to be the things which are probably different from our Islamic attitude.

For more explanation of this concept, which is particular to the monotheistic cultures, we present an introduction. We said that the fulfillment of the duties and being bound over the responsibilities is a general value. Now let us see what these responsibilities are and who is the one who calls to account for these responsibilities?

Usually, the responsibilities are divided into three groups, of which two groups have universal acceptance and one group is particular to the religious and theist communities. As for the responsibilities which have been accepted in all human communities, one is responsibility towards the community, so that if individuals do not fulfill them, they will be called to account, and the other is towards the conscience of the individual himself, namely, everybody has certain duties towards his conscience which he should fulfill even if the society does not call him to account. In the midst of this, there is another kind of responsibility, too, which is just accepted in godly communities and that is the responsibility towards Allah and naturally those people submit to it who believes in Allah.

But if we view the matter with a wider outlook, we will see that we (on the basis of the divine outlook in Islam) have just one kind of responsibility and that is just towards Allah, of which the cases are however different, not that there are numerous ones who call to account for them. It is Allah, Who has created man's existence, has granted him the blessings and has endowed him with social life, intellect and conscience.

So, the true caller to account is Allah and all responsibilities are towards Him, but their cases are different. Sometimes Allah calls to account for the duties which He Himself has ordained as 'ibadah (acts of worship), for example, He calls a person to account and asks him why he has not performed the wajib salawat or why he has not fulfilled the other act(s) of worship.

Also, sometimes Allah calls one to account for the duties He has ordered regarding His (other) servants, for example, he asks: "Why did not you observe My command regarding the poor?" Hence, the poor or the community themselves have no right upon the others and cannot call the others to account, unless Allah has permitted it.

The case of one kind of responsibilities is the individual himself, not that the individuals call one to account for it, e.g., Allah asks: "Why did you oppress yourself?" If a person attempts a suicide or any other action which is a proof of oppression to one' self, Allah calls the person to account for the same and asks him: "Why did you oppress yourself'?" again the one who calls to account and who holds responsible is Allah. So, on the basis of At-Tawhid (monotheistic) view, all responsibilities are basically towards the Almighty Allah.

The Basis of Responsibility

Taking into consideration the above matters, the question arises as to what is the basis of responsibility and how is it that Allah calls us to account? This is a technical discussion which should be propounded in the philosophy of ethics and in the philosophy of law. But here, we will just point out the secret of the solution of this matter.

Basically, the caller to account can be the one who is the owner of the case for which someone is to be called to account. If someone enters another one's house (without being permitted), the inmate of house can call the newly entered person to account in case the former is the owner of the house. As for the public properties of the society, too, because all are owners (of the same) to some proportion, they have the right to call to account. So, man can call to account when he has a right towards something and owns something.

As for us men, the same is the case, namely, the one who calls us to account should be the one who is the owner of us and the owner of the things which are at our disposal and who can say: "*Why, I granted you being and endowed you with a healthy body, why did you oppress this body?*"; "*Why, I gave you the power of meditation and intellect, why did not you use it in the proper way'?*" ; "*Why, I put clean air at your disposal, Why did you pollute it'?*" And all such accounts are called to by the one who is the owner; otherwise, there would be no right for calling to account.

Therefore, true ownership belongs to Allah and it is just He Who has the right to call to account, to ordain duties and hold responsible and Whom we are truly owned by, so that this being owned is never negated, contrary to nominal cases of being owned which are negotiable and transferable, such as the house, the car or the dress which you own, but which on selling them, you no longer own them.

This is a nominal ownership which is both vanishable and transferable and among the things which the Almighty Allah cannot do, one is this very fact that He cannot release His servants from servitude (to Him)! Because it is an impossible matter. Allah cannot drive any being out of being His creatures and say: You are no longer owned by me and neither are you My creature. As long as anything exists in the world, us being are the same as being the creature of/and owned by Allah and coming out of being owned means to become nothing.

Creational and Divine Legislative 'Ibadah

Taking into consideration this outlook which takes form on the basis of At-Tawhid, each movement of the creatures is the emergence of an effect from servitude to Allah, because its being in existence is the same as being owned (by Allah). The heat and the light which emanate from the sun, the breeze which blows, the rain which falls, the plant which grows and the flowers and fruits which appear on the trees are effects of all these beings being owned and are indicators that the manner of creation and planning are of the same.

Hence, all the movements of the beings can be regarded as a creational 'ibadah (a creational servitude to Allah); that is, any being, willy-nilly, whatever effect emerges out of it, has manifested a

At-Tawhid: Monotheism

sign of it being owned by - and its servitude to - the Almighty Allah. In the Holy Qur'an, it has been said that all beings praise Allah and there are even a number of suwar which begin with the following sentences:

"Whatever is in the heavens and whatever is in the earth declares the glory of Allah... (64:1)."

In other verses of the Holy Qur'an, it has been said that all things make sajdah (prostration) to Allah, even the shadows which fall on the ground:

"...Its (very) shadows return from right and left, making obeisance to Allah... (16:48)."

More delicate than these, the Holy Qur'an says that the sound of the thunder and the song of nightingales and the twitter of sweet-singing birds are all praise of Allah:

"And the thunder declares His glory with His praise, and the angels too are in awe of Him... (13:13)."

And finally, the most general ayah of the Holy Qur'an in this connection is the following:

their glorification... (17:44)."

At-Tawhid in the Ideological System of Islam

One of the interpretations made for this group of ayat is that they mean creational 'ibadah (worship), creational tasbih (praising, glorifying) and creational sujud (prostration); all the movements and the effects of their existence are signs of them being servants of and owned by the Almighty Allah which on one hand they manifest Allah's qualities of beauty and perfection and on the other hand, declare Allah's being free from defects, destruction, naught, and the negative qualities (the qualities which Allah is devoid of and which can never be attributed to Him).

That aspect which is demonstrative of the qualities of perfection (of Allah) is called hamd (praising Allah's qualities), and that aspect which is indicative of and which establishes transcendence of Allah from defects is called tasbih (praising Allah's transcendence over all defects) which is a creational 'ibadah (servitude) to Allah. The limbs of our bodies have this 'ibadah too. Our hands, without our will-power, praise Allah, our feet, without our will-power praise Allah, the same is true also of the other limbs and parts of our bodies. Yet, there is also a divine legislative and voluntary 'ibadah which is particular to men.

Although the free actions (the actions which we perform out of our own free will) in any form they might be, are also signs of servitude to Allah and are creational 'ibadah, but in terms of divine legislation and the sphere of selection and free choice, 'ibadah is applied to particular actions, A man, who is without 'ibadah (without servitude), does not and will not exist in the world, because the reality of his existence is being possessed (being owned) and is dominated by the powers which have surrounded him and which have affected his effects and movements.

In this midst, if he recognizes the true Effective One (Allah), learns the way to reach Him and moves in that very direction, he has made 'ibadah to Allah, but if he does not know Him (Allah) and docs not step in His path, he has not fulfilled divine legislative 'ibadah, Anyhow, man's conduct is a conduct of 'ibadah (a conduct of servitude), either 'ibadah to Allah or 'ibadah to the others; 'ibadah to the Shaytan (Satan), 'ibadah to one's self, 'ibadah to the self-made idols or 'ibadah to null beings which have no external reality at all.

In the Holy Qur'an, Allah says:

"Did I not charge you, O children of Adam! that you should not serve the shaytan? Surely he is your open enemy. And that you should serve Me; this is the right way (36:60-61)."

At-Tawhid in the Ideological System of Islam

In the above verses of the Holy Qur'an, Allah says that man is on two paths, one is the way of 'ibadah to Allah and the other is the way of 'ibadah to shaytan and Allah has advised the people to choose the way of 'ibadah to Him which leads to their felicity and perfection.

The point which is necessary to notice here is that the concept of 'ibadah in this sense is different from the meaning which is generally in our minds of 'ibadah and which is just applied to a series of acts of worship and values such as the wajib salawat, sawm and hajj (specified pilgrimage to Makkah according to the Islamic shari'ah). In the concept of 'ibadah in the extensive and general sense, all the free actions of man (all the actions which man fulfills out of free will) are 'ibadah.

Now, if such actions and conducts have favorable effects on man's felicity and perfection and are pleased at by Allah they become 'ibadah to Allah, but if they cause man's fall, decline and his gelling away from the (divinely ordained) end, they will be 'ibadah to shaytan and are rated as an anti-value. But in any way, they (man's free actions) are 'ibadah and anyhow, we are not outside either of the two conditions, we are either in 'ibadah to Allah or in 'ibadah to shaytan.

At-Tawhid: Monotheism

The conclusion derived from these preliminaries is that worshiping Allah and 'ibadah to Him, too, have general and value-related concepts in the Islamic culture, as is the case with taqwa, so that an action fulfilled by an individual, a group, or a society has value when the title of taqwa and the title of worshiping Allah correspond to it. Even if an action is, in terms of the other value systems praise worthy and acceptable, but is not corresponded to by these two titles, in the value system of Islam it does not reach the necessary limit for value and is below the necessary limit. For example, helping the poor and the weak is a value which has been more or less accepted in all the ethical systems or the world but in the value system of Islam it has no value in the abstract form and is generally regarded as a good action.

Yet, (in the Islamic value system) such actions reach the necessary level of value when they stem from the individual's faith, are fulfilled out of divine motive (out of motive of winning Allah's pleasure) and in one word, it has goodness of action (in accordance with Allah's command) and goodness of the doer having free will (divine motive), otherwise if it is merely regarded as an emotional matter, it will not be of much value and will not reach the necessary level of value either, because such emotion more or less exists in animals too, particularly the motherly emotion and the emotion of supporting one's kind which is observed in, for example, ravens too; therefore, it cannot be the only criterion for value.

Criticism on A Theory

This matter is in fact a response to one of the great foundations of the philosophy of ethics which is today prevalent in Western countries and which due to our Islamic insight being not very strong, has unfortunately more or less spread and penetrated among some groups of our society too. Many of the philosophers of ethics in Western countries regard the criterion for value to be serving the others and love for the others and say if an action is performed for the sake of personal benefit and with individual motive, it has no value and/or it is anti-value, but if it is performed with the motive of loving the others it will be desirable and of value.

Some of our intellectuals too who have had discussions and writings in the field of ethics, have sought the relationship of At-Tawhid with the philosophy of ethics just here and have imagined that At-Tawhid means that man melts himself in the society and instead of "1" always says "We" and always takes "We" into consideration.

This matter is objectionable in the Islamic outlook from numerous viewpoints:

The first objection: The first objection is that At-Tawhid has no concern with the social "I" and "We". In the previous discussions we have fully clarified that At- Tawhid, as an Islamic concept, means belief in the One God in the dimension of creativity, creational Lordship, Divine Legislative Lordship and in (Allah's) Being the (Only) Worshiped. At-Tawhid is not a sociological and psychological concept; rather it is a theological and philosophical concept, that is to know God as One and Only and to believe in His Oneness and to put this belief into effect in action. So, man's melting or not melting himself in the society has nothing to do with At-Tawhid as an Islamic concept.

The second objection: It is that the criterion for value is not just love for the others, Many of our actions are performed with individual motive and yet are of very high value. That faithful servant (of Allah) who gets up at mid-night in winters from the warm bed and engages in 'ibadah to Allah on the cold and coarse carpet of the Mosque and starts supplicating and praying to Allah, is his action individual or social? Is this action performed out of the motive of serving the society or for attaining the good of the hereafter and spiritual and eternal good of the individual himself'? Whereas the Holy Qur'an cites such persons with a very exalted interpretation and at the loftiest level of value and says:

> "So no soul knows what is hidden for them of that which will refresh the eyes... (32:17)."

No one knows what felicity and joy the Almighty Allah has provided for such persons. Allah will give them such a great reward that no man's mind can think of. So, it is not the case that values arc confined to serving the others or, as there is a famous saying "'ibadah is nothing but serving Allah's creatures."

The third objection: It is that not every love for others is valuable and at least it does not have the necessary amount for value. We have already expressed that caring for others is also observed among ravens, monkeys and in many other animals. But it is not the case that the emotion of care for the others is by itself sufficient for man's action and man's soul to attain value, rather they will be of value if they are with divine motive and this is not exclusive to emotion either. The satisfaction of instincts, with divine motive is 'ibadah to Allah too.

Eating, drinking and even sexual intercourse, if fulfilled with divine motive, are also 'ibadah. So, the only criterion (according to Islam) is that firstly, the action is to be approved by Allah (be in accordance with Allah's commands) and secondly, to be with a divine motive and the intention of getting close to Allah (winning Allah's pleasure). In one of the stages already expressed: fear of punishment, covet for reward and hope for meeting Allah and winning His pleasure.

Clarification of the Ethical Theory of Islam

A significant matter to be noticed here and to be reasonably and philosophically clarified and justified is how human behavior and permanent qualities become possessed of value ·through 'ibadah to Allah and perfect obedience and humbling oneself before Allah? In this regard, from the outlook of Islam and the ayat of the Holy Qur'an and the riwayat, we have no doubt, for the Almighty Allah says:

"And I have not created the jinn and the men except that they should worship Me (51:56)."

The only aim of creation of man and of jinn who from the viewpoint of the Holy Qur'an are two kinds of responsible (entrusted with duties) beings is just (their) serving the One God (Allah - The One and Only). Of course taking into consideration other ayat (of the Holy Qur'an) we come to realize that this is not the final goal, this very 'ibadah for Allah in another ayah of the Holy Qur'an, has been propounded as the right way.

"And that you should serve Me; this is the right way (36:61)."

Worship Allah, this is the right way. The same thing which in the former ayah (56:51) had been mentioned as the aim or creation, has been introduced as the right way in the latter (6:36), meaning that 'ibadah is a medium goal and above it there is another goal. That very act of 'ibadah itself has been considered for a higher goal and that is attaining nearness to the Almighty Allah (attaining Allah's pleasure) in which all human virtues and perfections are summed up.

But for this theory to be presentable and defendable in the face of the other ethical and value theories of the world and particularly so that our educated youth will be able to defend the righteous position of Islam before other schools of thought, it is necessary to clarify this theory on the basis of intellectual reasons and philosophical proofs. The principles which are necessary for the clarification of this mailer arc three basic principles.

At-Tawhid: Monotheism

The First Principle

It is that the criterion for the goodness and value of the action is the effect which a free conduct has on man's spiritual and intellectual perfection. For the clarification of this basic principle which is of the significant matters of the philosophy of ethics in the scientific and philosophical circles of the world, we express an analysis on the concept of value and anti-value and their equivalent in the Islamic culture, namely, "good" and "evil".

We regard certain things as goad and also accept certain things as evil. For instance, all of us regard health to be good, rate knowledge, power and ability as good and opposite to them, regard sickness, being malformed, being ignorant, disabled and powerless to be evil. Philosophers have conducted a wise analysis on this concept and have come to the conclusion that the common aspect among all these goods consists of the perfection of the being and the common aspect among all these evils consists of the imperfection of the being.

For instance, when we compare an ignorant man with a learned man, we observe that the learned man has a perfection which the ignorant man lacks. So, the being of the learned man is more perfect than the being of the ignorant man, and/or since a sick man does not have the power to defend against diseases and cannot confront aggressive microbes and loses his body's balance, his being is imperfect compared to a healthy person.

A brave man, in various phases, can achieve his goals, but a timid and cowardice cannot. Then they (the philosophers) have gone further and with a more careful analysis have come to the conclusion that perfection is a stage of being and imperfection is a stage of non-being and is a matter of non-being.

Hence, we can regard being (existence) as equal to good, since it is being (existence) and regard non-being (non-existence) to be evil, since it is non-being (non-existence). Therefore, the good of every being is its perfection and tile evil of every being is its imperfection.

Sometimes the perfection of a being causes the imperfection of another being. The burning effect of the fire is the perfection of the fire, but if it falls into a harvest, it causes the destruction of the harvest. The cutting effect of knives and swords is their perfection, but when they come into contact with the body of an innocent man, they cause his death.

A microbe has perfection since it is a living being, but this very microbe, when it enters our bodies, it may afflict us with diseases and cause an

At-Tawhid: Monotheism

imperfection for us. Maulawi, the great gnostic and poet has famous poems in which it is said that poison is good for the snake itself, but bad for the one who is stung by the snake.

Also sometimes the opposite is the case, A matter may be a non-existence, imperfection and in itself evil, but becomes good and the cause of perfection for another thing. You enter a garden and see a gardener cutting of the branches and leaves of a tree, but if you are not aware of the gardening works, you will think that the gardener is doing work which is bad, cutting off the branches and leaves of the tree which arc apparently being and perfection for the tree.

But if you are aware of the matters related to gardening, you know that the gardener cuts off some of the extra branches (which hinder the growth of the tree) so that the tree will grow more. Here, the non- existence of these branches is an imperfection and non-existence matter, but for the tree it is considered to be good and causes the tree to grow better.

Now let us see what the superiority of perfections depend on?

We start this matter from plants. In your opinion, in comparison, which one is more perfect, a walnut tree or a plain tree? You certainly think a walnut tree is more perfect. Why? Because a walnut tree has something more than the plain tree and that is the fruit it (the walnut tree) bears. Therefore, since it has more effects of existence, it is more perfect. Comparison is in the same manner between two walnut trees.

That walnut tree is more perfect of which the final result and fruit is more, and the same is true of the walnut tree which is of less size but which gives more fruit, compared to the walnut tree which occupies more size, but has little fruit. Now let us compare an animal with a tree. Can the criterion for superiority be regarded to be the size of the animal? If it were so, a plain tree would be a thousand times more perfect than a nightingale.

But it definitely is not so. Because a nightingale has something's more than a plant (something's which a plant lacks), namely, besides us physical growth, it has senses and (the ability of) voluntary movement. It is the nightingale which on seeing a flower starts twittering and in which a feeling and sense emerge, a sense which a plain tree will never have.

So the criterion for the superiority of a nightingale to a tree is not bigger for either being. But if we also compare two animals with each other, that animal which has more sense and stronger understanding is more perfect, not that one which is bigger in size, like an Arabian horse and a rhinoceros. An Arabian horse has more wits, has better leaping, is capable of performing more useful work and is more loyal than a rhinoceros, but a rhinoceros is just big in size.

Now let us consider a man. If we want to compare a man with trees and animals, what should we consider his superiority to be? Which one is more perfect, a man or a plain tree? Is a man more perfect or an elephant? Man's superiority to plants and animals is not in having more bodily growth, more physical power, more passions (carnal desires), greater power of defense and/or even more animal perceptions; these do not contribute to human perfection. If these were the criterion, then animals would be by far ahead of us and is this not selfish of us that since we regard ourselves more perfect, we should look for another criterion! This is a truly philosophical matter).

Rather what makes man superior to and more perfect than the animals and other beings is that human and divine soul of his which constitutes the proof for the following ayat of the Holy Qur'an:

"...And I breathed into him of My spirit... (15:29 and 38:72)."

and,

"...So blessed be Allah, the best of the creators (23:14)."

The question which is raised here is that, is the value just in the superiority of man's spiritual perfections or arc plant and animal perfections also of value?

Let us consider an apple tree. In an apple tree, taking root, turning green, bearing branches, leaves and even blossoms are considered perfection insofar as they cause bearing fruit, otherwise they will not be of value. These kinds of perfections are preliminary perfections which are not of value in themselves, rather they are preliminaries for eventual and genuine perfection, and value is acquired through them.

In man it is also true. If a growth emerges in the body by itself and does not cause that main, basic and eventual growth, it is an animal growth and will not be of any value for man from the viewpoint that he is man. A healthy body is valuable for man in case he uses it for his spiritual and intellectual progress, not if he misuses his health - using it for hurting others.

The same is true of other qualities too. For example, bravery is desirable from the Islamic viewpoint when it is used in the way of man's spiritual and intellectual perfection and in the way of getting near to the Almighty Allah (winning Allah's pleasure and favor), otherwise 'Amr ibn 'Abd Wadd (the great (notorious) enemy of Islam) and some others like him were also brave and had this animal value.

The superiority of a brave man, apart from his spiritual goal and perfection to another man is like the superiority of a rhinoceros to a horse and the superiority of an elephant to a gazelle. This preliminary perfection will be of value when it is used in the way of attaining that eventual human perfection, when it has been achieved for that and used in the way of attaining it (eventual human perfection). Justice, too, which in today's world culture has absolute value, in the view of the Holy Qur'an, it is valuable since it is a preliminary stage for getting closer to taqwa:

"...Act equitably, that is nearer to piety... (5:8)."

Otherwise, this sense is found in some animals like the honey-bee, termite and some others too. This is not an absolute human value. In the value system of Islam, justice is of value when it is in the way of Allah and for attaining a loftier goal and moves man towards that point of peak (that highest point of perfection).

The point which is necessary to be paid attention here is, the relationship between the philosophical good and the ethical good, but before clarifying this relationship, we will somewhat discuss about the good and the evil and their criterion.

Clarification of the Criterion for the Good and the Bad

One of the most disputed human matters in the course of the history of man's life has been the issue of the criterion for a good and bad action and good and evil. Today, many of the world's philosophical schools which have the great universities of the Western World under their domination, including the Positivists maintain that good and bad arc subjects to the persons' taste and inclination and that there is no reality beyond this like and dislike. In the Greek moral philosophy it was said that the criterion for value is moderation of three powers; the power of passion, the power of anger and the power of intellect.

But the question remains to be answered as to who says that moderation should be the criterion for goodness and badness. Eventually, the highest ethical school which the West presented was the ethics of Kant. Kant maintained moral axioms and stated that they are unquestionable; telling the truth is absolutely good and there is no condition for it either, it is a criterion itself. When asked in case telling the truth causes an innocent man to be killed, should one still tell the truth?" Kant replied: *"One should tell the truth, this is an absolute value."* This is the zenith of the Western thinking in the clarification of the philosophy of ethics. But Islam says: *"Basically, action is a means not an end."*

A free action is performed for an end and receives its value from that end. In the philosophy of the morality of Islam, good is an action which drives man towards his eventual perfection, namely getting near Allah and bad is an action which drives man away from that end (i.e., from attaining nearness to Allah) and from this it becomes clear why in Islam so much emphasis is laid on niyyah (intention); well, in fact it is man's niyyah which gives direction to his action.

As for the relationship between philosophical good and ethical good, ethical good is propounded in relation to man's free conducts and actions and there is a good which is a means, because it is a quality for action and the nature of action is a means for the result and the end; but as for the desired result, it is not an ethical concept, rather it is a philosophical topic.

So, the ethical good is in one sense other than philosophical good, but is however not separate from it either and there is a cause and effect relationship between these two, and in other words, ethical good is preamble for philosophical good, Therefore, when we say that good action causes perfection for man's soul, the goodness of the action is an ethical concept, but the perfection of the soul is a philosophical concept.

The Second Principle

In the clarification of the criterion for the evaluation of actions is the fact that perfection of the soul which man should attain through (good) free actions is nearness to Allah (winning Allah's pleasure and favor).

About the meaning and concept of this qurb (nearness) to Allah, various statements and views have been expressed about each one of which we will give some explanation to the extent necessary.

Various Meanings and Cases of the Application of Qurb

The first concept which in common conversations is applied about 'qurb' is qurb in terms of place. For example, as when two persons are seated near or in proximity to each other, 'this person is near that person and/or this person is away from that person'. Is man's being near to Allah in this sense? where (in the Holy Qur'an) Asiyah - the wife or Fir'awn (pharaoh) says:

> "...My Lord! Build for me a house with Thee in the garden... (66:11)."

Did she (by saying so) mean that a faithful person attains nearness of a place with Allah in Paradise? Those who know even the fundamentals of the Islamic beliefs will know that nearness to Allah is definitely not in this sense, because nearness of a place is imagined among objects and Allah is not an object to have a place, to Whom another object becomes near or from Whom another object gets away. So, getting near to Allah does not mean nearness of a place.

One of the other cases (of the application) of qurb in our conversations is the nearness in terms of time. About two persons living in a time close to each other it is said that they are qaribul-'asr (near in terms of time), vis-a-vis two beings, two individuals and/or two societies which have great time distance, one has been living thousands of years ago and the other is living today, about them it is said that they are away from each other.

It is obvious that man's getting near Allah is not in terms of time either, because firstly Allah does not have a time, rather He encompasses all times, just as He has no place and is available at all places. Besides, being near and/or being away in terms of time and place in themselves do not create any perfection. Anyhow, nearness in terms of place and time is impossible with regard to the Almighty Allah and getting near Him in these two definitions is false. So, how is man to get near Allah?

One other kind of qurb which we have in common conversations is that two things arc compared with each other in respect of resemblance in specification, perfections and characteristics apart from time and place. In this sense can it be said that man gets near Allah? Does qurb to Allah mean that more resemblance to Allah is achieved? Some have attempted to interpret qurb to Allah in this way, but in reality this sense is incorrect too. because firstly, Allah does not resemble anything, (as the Holy Qur'an says):

> *"...Nothing is like a likeness of Him... (42:11)."*

and that sometimes the interpretation of "being like God" is applied, is a neglectful interpretation. Secondly, this comparison is where two beings are independent of each other. For example, when we compare two learned men with each other and say that the knowledge of this learned man is near that of the other learned mall, none of these is dependent on and/or the ray of the other, rather each one of them is independent of the other, this learned man has a knowledge for himself and the other learned man has a knowledge for himself, we compare these two knowledge together and say this one is near that one.

Such a comparison between man and Allah is not proper, because man has nothing independent of Allah and all he has is from Allah. Thirdly, Allah's perfection is infinite and each being, at least in the stage of existence has a phase of finiteness and limitation, and never the finite is comparable with the infinite. If you consider a line with a length of one meter and ask what proportion docs this one meter line have with an infinite line, those who are even a little conversant with mathematics know that the answer to this question is that there is no proportion between the finite and the infinite.

At-Tawhid in the Ideological System of Islam

Now if Instead of a one meter line a two-meter line is put, again the answer is "nothing" and even if we draw a line as long as the distance between the earth and the sun, and it is asked that what proportion does this line have to an infinite line, again the answer will he "nothing". No matter how much man attains perfection, he is after all limited and is not a party in proportion to Allah's infinite perfections, to be said about him that he has now got some what nearer to Allah.

Therefore, that some imagine that when man's perfection becomes more, his difference with Allah becomes less and in this sense he gets nearer to Allah, is due to short-sightedness in knowing Allah. Such comparisons can be assumed between objects and the beings which are independent of each other which do not have relation of existence with each other and one of which is not of the stages of the other and is not its effect, but between the existence-giving Cause and the effect such a comparison is totally wrong.

Also some have imagined that by qurb, it is meant just what the following verse of the Holy Qur'an refers to:

> "...And We are nearer to him than his life-vein (50:16)."

Namely, Allah is nearer to man than his life-vein.

Though this matter is true and no firmer and closer relationship between this (relation) can be assumed between Allah and His creatures, it is clear that this qurb and nearness is not particular to the believers and that it exists not only for all men, whether believers, or the disbelievers, the pious, the lewd, but it also exists for all creatures and all creatures have this relationship with Allah.

Sometimes qurb is also applied in the sense of honor and formality. For example, we say that such and such a person is near to such and such a minister and is favored by him, that is, they have friendly relations with each other and if the former has a request, the latter will not reject it and will listen to him. About man's qurb to Allah, too, sometimes interpretation is made in this way, that man gets so near to Allah in the sense that Allah heeds his words, pays attention to his requests and hears his prayers.

Among these five meanings, only the last-mentioned meaning conforms to qurb of Allah, a qurb which is attained through worship and obedience to the Almighty Allah, as is said in a hadithun-qudsiyy.

> *"A servant (of Allah) owing to servitude (to Allah) attains such a position where the Almighty Allah becomes his hearing ears, his seeing eyes and his mighty hands."*[19]

A servant (of Allah) owing to servitude (to Allah) attains such a position that in accordance with the interpretation of the above hadith, the Almighty Allah becomes his hearing car, his seeing eye and his capable hand and it is clear that the prayer of such a servant (of Allah) will be heard (by Allah) and that the Almighty Allah will secure his needs and wants.

But the question (which may be raised here) is that is such a position just an honorary and formal position or is it an existential and true perfection? And our reply is that this position of qurb to Allah is a true perfection for human soul and that to become mustajabud-du'wah (one whose prayer is heard by Allah) and even the acceptance of one's intercession for the others with Allah are of the effects of this spiritual perfection, not that they are merely a credit and an agreement and in other words, the true meaning of qurb to Allah is the sixth meaning which we will now explain to the extent the situation demands.

---

[19] Al-'Usul al-Kafi, vol. 2, p. 352.

For the clarification of this meaning, we should point out two noble philosophical matters, the details of which should be sought in their own place and in the related books.

The First Matter

The existence of each creature has a relation between itself and the Creator and no creature has any independence of the existence-giving Creator and this is a matter of clarification which is rated among the honors of the great Islamic expert Sadrul-Muta'allihin Ash-Shirazi and the philosophical expression of the fourth meaning of the above-mentioned meanings is also based on this very matter, that is, the reason why the Almighty Allah is nearer to each being than any other thing is the very fact that the existence of each creature has a relation itself to and dependence on Him (the Creator) and if this relation is cut off, it will no longer have any existence; it can be said that the existence of each creature in relation to the Almighty Allah is like the existence of a subjective figure for man which if set aside, will have no existence any longer and certainly the relation of the beings with the Almighty Allah is by far stronger than this example.

The Second Matter

It is that the existence of the soul is of the category of the existence of science and in other words; just as the requisite for each physical existence is "extension", the requisite for each abstract existence is also "knowledge" which requisite is of course not anything outside the existence of the soul.

Taking into consideration these two matters, we conclude that whenever the existence of man's soul becomes more perfect, his knowledge will become more perfect. The first stage of the perfection of the soul is attaining "self-awareness" and when one's self-awareness becomes perfect, he will find the reality of his existence which is the same as relation, belonging to and dependence on the Almighty Allah, namely, he will attain "self-awareness" and it is for this reason that in the Islamic culture "self-awareness" and "God-awareness" are coupled together. On the one hand, it has been said that:

> *"Anybody who knew himself knew his Lord."*

and on the other hand, the Holy Qur'an says:

> *"...Those who forsook Allah, so He made them forsake their own souls... (59:19)."*

Those who forsook themselves become afflicted with Allah's forsaking.

At-Tawhid: Monotheism

So, an inseparable relation exists between knowing one's self and knowing Allah and also between forsaking one's self and Allah's forsaking. The reality of "forsaking oneself" and "self-alienation" in the Islamic culture is this very matter that a person forgets his human identity and his attention is so diverted to this world's luxuries and pleasures that he forsakes his reality and his human perfection and felicity, namely, he forgets about his relation to and dependence on the Almighty Allah.

The conclusion is this, that true perfection of man's soul is God-awareness (awareness of Allah) which has innumerable stages and the more man's celestial soul becomes perfect, the more his awareness of Allah will increase and this awareness of one's self and of one's God is the same as the existence of the soul.

Therefore, man's eventual perfection is his attaining perfect awareness and his innate and intuitive knowledge (knowledge acquired not through the five senses, but through illumination of one's heart) about the Almighty Allah and this awareness about Allah is the very true qurb to Allah which should be attained through efforts and endeavors. Therefore the true meaning of qurb to Allah as an acquired perfection for man's soul consists of intuitive and inner qurb, and the realization of this fact that man's existence is nothing but relation and attachment to the Almighty Allah, and that it is not merely knowledge and acquired learning which are attained through concepts and by way of intellectual reasoning.

The Third Principle

The clarification of the moral and value theory of Islam says that this perfection and qurb to Allah is attained just in the light of the conducts the general title of which is 'ibadah, worshiping Allah, and virtuousness. To prove this principle from the philosophical point of view, too, requires a technical and complicated expression which does not suit this discussion. However, we will try to explain, with a simple expression this principle, too.

We came to know that the Almighty Allah is not a physical and place-occupying being whom we could get near to with the movement of the body and traversing material distance and that no kind of physical action and reaction and body change and development can in itself have any role in changing man's relation to the Almighty Allah and that the truth of man's qurb to Allah is inner and intuitive nearness and attaining man's existential relationship with Him.

Taking into consideration these points it can easily be accepted that what plays the main role in man's getting near to the Almighty Allah is that very man's power of perceiving and witnessing, namely, the truth of his soul which in many cases is called "heart" and the free (voluntary) relationship which is established between man's heart and the Almighty Allah is by means of attention (to Allah), this very attention itself is termed "dhikr (remembrance of Allah) of the heart" and when this attention and remembrance become the source of performance of an action and a conduct, it is rated as the niyyah (intention) and motive for the action, and since the perfection of man's soul and spirit is attained by means of free actions and each kind of conducts can have a role in the promotion or regression of the soul in one of its dimensions, therefore we conclude that man's all-sided perfection is attained when all distinguished conducts are fulfilled with divine motive, and the main stimulant and the giver of direction to conduct is attention to Allah (swt).

In other words, just as physical forces determine the direction of the movement of the objects, so also psychic motives which stem from attention to and remembrance of Allah are spiritual forces which determine the spiritual direction of man's actions and conducts and which give value to them and as already explained, such conducts have two general terms in the Islamic culture: one is taqwa in its general sense and the other 'ibadah in its general sense.

The conclusion is that each free action to the extent it enjoys divine intention and motive will have a positive value; and to the extent it stems from ungodly, egoistic and polytheistic intention it will have a negative value. Thus, the role of At-Tawhid in the value system of Islam becomes clear.

Quranic Expressions About the Philosophy of Morality

So far, we have explained the theory of Islam in the philosophy of morality and values with the simplest rational expressions which were possible for us. Now we cite some examples of Quranic expressions concerning the principles of this theory:

In Surat ush-Shams (Surah 91 of the Holy Qur'an) in the wake of a number of ayat in which the Almighty Allah swears by the sun, by the moon, by the night, by the day and the like, He says:

"And the soul and Him Who made it perfect, Then He inspired it to understand what is right and wrong for it; He will indeed be successful who purifies it, And he will indeed fail who corrupts it (91:7-10)."

Of the many points inferred from these ayat, we content ourselves with citing three points:

The First Point: is that Allah swears by human soul, the soul which Allah has made and delivered well and among all creatures man has a particular privilege to determine his destiny with his own free will: to choose either the way of felicity and salvation or the way of adversity and corruption and certainly Allah's goal of the creation of man is that he attains felicity and salvation, but since human felicity is a matter to be attained by the way of man's own will-power and free choice, so there should necessarily exist another point in the face of it too towards which would retrogress of his own ill-choice anybody who chooses to.

The Second Point: is that selection of either of the two points - exaltation and perfection or fall and retrogression demands recognition. Because it is obvious that without awareness and recognition proper selection and choice does not take place. Hence, the Almighty Allah has made two general ways known to man: one the way of taqwa and the other the way of fur, and from this very interpretation it is inferred that the criterion for the positive conduct values is "taqwa" and the criterion for the negative moral values is fur, as was already explained in the foregoing expressions.

The Third Point: is that to traverse the way of taqwa is the very "purification of the soul" and its result is the growth and perfection of the soul, just as to traverse the way of fur is the very pollution of the soul, the result of which is the fall and destruction of the soul itself. So man, by selecting the way of taqwa, gives growth and perfection to his soul and by selecting the way of fur and license pollutes and destroys his own soul.

Therefore, the result of man's free conducts, be they in the direction of growth and perfection or in the direction of fall and retrogression, will accrue to man himself, and from here it can well be inferred that the value conducts have true effect on the perfection and imperfection of the soul, and that the positive or negative value criterion is this very perfection and imperfection of man's soul and this is that very first principle in the expression of the logical reason we referred to previously.

From another set of the ayat of the Holy Qur'an it is inferred that man's eternal felicity and adversity is the result of his own faith and infidelity and praiseworthy and indecent actions:

> "And that man shall have nothing but what he strives for (53:39)."

> "...For it, what it has earned, and against it what it has incurred... (2:286)."

> "...And every soul is paid of whatever it has earned (3:25)."

> "The day when every soul shall find present what it has done of good... (3:30)."

And there are tens of other ayat in the Holy Qur'an indicating that the blessings and torments in the Hereafter are the result of the actions which man has himself fulfilled in this world, rather they are those very actions of his which would in the hereafter world appear in the form of blessing or torment.

Of course the language of most of the ayat of the Holy Qur'an is that the blessings or torments in the Hereafter are the reward or punishment for the conducts in this world. With our mind having got acquainted with the concepts of reward and punishment, it might at first be imagined that the relation of good and bad actions with their hereafterly results is a nominal and conventional relation, but taking into view the cited ayat of the Holy Qur'an it becomes clear that beyond these nominal concepts a series of creational facts and true and real relations are hidden, though our knowledge is not sufficient for the discovery of these true relations, because we have no experience of such relations.

Included among the ayat to be considered in this discussion are the ayat which have mentioned about spiritual light and darkness, which terms have been largely applied with regard to truth and falsehood, moral and value, good and evil and with regard to the affairs related to them in the Holy Qur'an and also in the sayings of the Holy Prophet (SA) of Islam and the Infallible Imams (AS) and which have a particular position in Islamic culture.

On one hand, the Holy Qur'an introduces the Almighty Allah as "nur (the light) of the heavens and the earth" and it is obvious that by this light, the generally known physical light is not meant and on the other hand, the Holy prophet (SA) of Islam has been introduced (by the Holy Quran) as:

"...A light-giving torch (33:46)."

and on the other hand the Holy Qur'an has itself been named "nur" (light):

At-Tawhid: Monotheism

> "...There has come to you light and a clear Book from Allah (5:15)."

And also the aim of the revelation of the Holy Qur'an to the Holy Prophet (SA) of Islam has been considered (by the Holy Qur'an) to be taking the people out of darkness and bringing them into the "light":

> "...that you may bring forth men, by their Lord's permission from utter darkness into light... (14:1)."

Also, the believers have been introduced (by the Holy Qur'an) as those who in this world arc possessed of light (nur), versus the infidels and those who are disobedient to Allah's commands who have sunk into darkness:

> "Is he who was dead then We raised him to life and made for him a light by which he walks among the people, like him whose likeness is that of one in utter darkness whence he cannot come forth?... (6:122)."

Finally, among the descriptions or the Resurrection Day, the Holy Qur'an says:

> "On that day you will see the faithful men and the faithful women— their light running before them and on their right hand—... (57:12)."

> "On the day when the hypocritical men and the hypocritical women will say to those who believe: Wait for us, that we may have light from your light; it shall be said: Turn back and seek a light (hinting that for seeking light you should return to the world which is impossible)... (57:13)."

And the most comprehensive ayat in this connection are ayat 35 to 40 of Surat un-Nur (Chapter 24) of the Holy Qur'an which start with this sentence:

"Allah is the light of the heavens and the earth... (24:35)."

And ends with this sentence:

"...And to whomsoever Allah does not give light, he has no light (24:40)."

Here, we do not helve the time to completely interpret and explain these ayat, but for the clarification of their relationship with the present discussion, we have to give a brief explanation:

In these ayat, after the Almighty Allah has been introduced as the light of the heavens and of the earth (the light of the worlds), a parable has been given for His light in ayah 35 of surah 24.

> *"...A likeness of His light is as a niche in which is a lamp, the lamp is in a glass, (and) the glass is as it were a brightly shining star, lit from a blessed olive-tree, neither eastern nor western... (24:35)."*

(Hinting that the sun shines from all its sides perfectly and no unripe fruit remains in it). Such oil is so susceptible for being inflamed that it is as if it automatically is lit without any fire reaching it.

About this parable many sayings have been expressed by the exegetists who we are unable to survey here. One of such commentaries is that the proof of this torch which is; ready to he kindled is the heart of a mu'min person which has the perfect aptitude for a relationship with the Almighty Allah and is enjoying the divine light. The other ayat confirm this view:

> *"In houses which Allah has permitted to be exalted and that His name may be remembered in them; there glorify Him therein in the mornings and the evenings, men whom neither merchandise nor selling diverts from the remembrance of Allah... (24:36-37)."*

In fact, it is the remembrance of Allah which makes their (godly men's) lives lit and luminous and which gives value to all their conducts and deeds.

At-Tawhid in the Ideological System of Islam

On the opposite side of these, there are the disbelievers. who due to forgetting Allah have sunk into darkness and whose actions have become null and valueless. And in the two last-mentioned verses, two parables have been cited for the actions of the disbelievers; The first parable is:

"...The mirage in a desert, which the thirsty man deems to be water; until when he comes to it he finds it to be naught, and there he finds Allah, so He pays back to him his reckoning in full... (24:39)."

That is, the disbelievers engage in efforts and endeavor in hope of felicity and attach their hearts to their own deeds, but when they should derive benefit from these efforts (in the Hereafter), they see no useful thing and the Almighty Allah will make it clear to them that they have done no useful work for their felicity.

The second parable for the disbeliever and the value of their deeds is:

"...Utter darkness in the deep sea: there covers it a wave above which is another wave, above which is a cloud, (layers of) utter darkness one above another; when he holds out his hand, he is almost unable to see it... (24:40)."

At-Tawhid: Monotheism

The above ayah ends with the following sentence:

> "...*And to whomsoever Allah does not give light, he has no light (24:40).*"

Whatever ambiguity, if any, might exist about the reality (the true meaning) of "misbah" (lamp), "zujajah" (glass) and "mishkat" (niche) (the expressions applied in surah 24 of the Holy Qur'an, in ayah 35 referred to) and whatever discussion, if any, might he made regarding the sea, the waves and the clouds surrounding it, there is no room for any doubt and ambiguity about this matter that these ayat regard the men of Allah (the believers) to be those who are blessed with light and felicity, who through their remembrance of Allah and heart-fell attention to the Creator make their lives valuable and that the disbelievers, through forgetting Allah, destroy the value of their deeds and will finally be afflicted with darkness and adversity.

So, the criterion for good, felicity, light and true value is the relation with the original source of light which is attained by means of faith in Allah and the attention of one's heart to Him and the criterion for evil, adversity, darkness, valueless and futility is the lack of relationship and connection with the original source of light which develop as a result of disbelief (in Allah), forgetting Allah and turning away from

www.ingramcontent.com/pod-product-compliance
Lightning Source LLC
Chambersburg PA
CBHW021441070526
44577CB00002B/237

His remembrance, like an electric light which on connection with the electricity-generating system is lit and on disconnection is extinguished. And these are the purports of those very principles to which in the last expression of logical reason we referred and thus the conformity of the expression of logical reason with the Quranic expressions becomes manifest.

Here, we end our discussion and beseech the Almighty Allah to deliver all of us from the various kinds of darkness's, to strengthen our relation and connection with the origin of Light, to protect all of us against any sort of deviation and unsound judgment and to finally associate us with His worthy servants and the pure lights of Ahlul-Bayt (AS) The Infallible and the Purified.

May greetings and Allah's blessings and mercy be upon you all.